History and Beliefs of
MORMONISM

Temple Square, Salt Lake City, Utah

History and Beliefs of
MORMONISM

by
Einar Anderson

KREGEL PUBLICATIONS
Grand Rapids, Michigan 49501

History and Beliefs of Mormonism by Einar Anderson, Copyright © 1981 by Kregel Publications, a division of Kregel, Inc. All rights reserved.

Some portions of the author's earlier work *I Was A Mormon* (Grand Rapids: Zondervan © 1964), now out of print, are included in this book.

First revised edition 1981
Reprinted 1985

Library of Congress Cataloging in Publication Data

Anderson, Einar, 1909-
  History and Beliefs of Mormonism.

  Revision of: *Inside Story of Mormonism.* Grand Rapids: Kregel Publications, 1973.
  1. Mormon Church—Doctrinal and controversial works.   I. Title.
BX8645.A67   1981   230'.933   81-13671
ISBN 0-8254-2122-5 (pbk.)   AACR2

Contents

Acknowledgements

The author wishes to gratefully acknowledge every source of information referred to, and any which may inadvertently be omitted.

I am deeply indebted to Mrs. Robert Fitch, my research and editorial assistant, for her valuable help in correcting the proofs and her many helpful suggestions.

To author Gordon Fraser and the Utah Christian Tract Society (La Mesa, California) and to Mr. and Mrs. Jerald Tanner, who have left the LDS Church. He was born and reared in the Mormon faith and has testified that he was nineteen years old before he heard the Word of Christ preached. Sandra Tanner, his wife, is a great, great granddaughter of Brigham Young who decided to leave the LDS Church when she read some of Brigham Young's sermons in the *Journal of Discourses* in which the prophet dealt with the Blood Atonement and other Mormon doctrines. Mr. Tanner operates the Modern Microfilm Company (Salt Lake City), specializing in copying books and documents on Mormonism which have been suppressed or are out of print.

And to my wife, Ann Anderson, who carefully rechecked the manuscript, and for her assistance in preparing this book. She ministers with me in my travels in the States and abroad.

Introduction

The Church of Jesus Christ of Latter Day Saints (or the Mormon Church, which name the Mormons find quite acceptable, represents one of the fastest growing religions in the world today. Its members declare that they are neither Catholic nor Protestant. They consider and refer to non-Mormons as Gentiles.

For many years Mormons have held disproportionately large numbers of influential positions in state and national politics, including many national Cabinet offices throughout several administrations. For this reason and because of its material wealth, the Mormon Church has succeeded in gaining prestige and power and is now recognized in many places as an orthodox Christian organization.

The Mormon Church presents a subtly appealing program. Its missionaries in their proselyting work (which word *they* use) are encompassing the globe, propagating their religion by using Christian terminology and biblical phraseology. For this reason many uninformed persons are deceived into thinking that Mormonism is part of traditional Christianity; whereas, Mormon doctrine, when examined, denies many of the Christian doctrines.

The purpose of this book is to give the reader a basis of little known facts concerning Mormon history and to offer examination of Mormon doctrine in the light of Bible comparisons, in order to more clearly understand Mormonism.

EARLY UTAH HISTORY

Many Mormons believe that Utah, particularly the Great Salt Lake Valley, was discovered by the Mormons. They believe this because their prophet Brigham Young declared it and even on the witness stand in a case in court, denied that the owners of Salt Lake lots derived title from the United States. He boldly asserted that the Emporium Corner was claimed by him "by right of discovery."

In October, 1879, J. R. McBride, Esq., a member of the Salt Lake Bar Association and one of the oldest pioneers of the area, wrote:

There are many Mormons who actually believe that this country was first discovered by the Mormon people. Brigham once, on the witness-stand, in a noted case pending in the courts, denied that the owners of lots in Salt Lake derived title from the United States, and boldly asserted that he claimed the Emporium Corner by "right of discovery."

Here are the facts. The valley of Great Salt Lake was as well known to travelers in the Far West — years before the Mormon chief squatted here to pass the winter of 1847, before resuming the journey to California — as the valley of the Sacramento, or that of the Williamette. It was no "desert," but a beautiful, grass-covered meadow, waiting to be appropriated. Its isolation was its protection, not its "sage-brush soil" or its "untamed savages." The labor of subduing it then was nothing, comparatively.

The writer was here before the Mormon settlement was made, and he knows that the pretense of reclaiming 'alkali soil' and subduing the Indians is utterly groundless. From Soda Springs to the headwaters of Salt Lake Valley to the South, there were not a hundred resident Indians. The Utes lived to the south and Bannocks to the north, and the settlers had nothing to do but to enter into and possess the land and work it to secure a fruitful result. One might as well talk of subduing or reclaiming the prairie soil of Illinois or Iowa as of "subduing" or "reclaiming" the lands of Utah.

There were miles upon miles of meadow lands, with grass mid-sides to a horse, where even irrigation was not required, when the saints (Mormons) came into the valley. All that was needed was ordinary industry.

I assert that the lands were, in the early settlement of Utah, more easily brought to bear fruitful returns than the ordinary wild lands of any of the Western States. All this talk and sentiment about the hardships of pioneering in Utah are pure fustian.

Those who crossed the plains when the writer did, anterior to the occupation of Utah, know that the real difficulties and dangers of that long journey were after we had passed Utah; the deserts of Nevada, the Snake Plains, the Alkali water, the alert and dangerous Indians were all to the west ... They "made the roads" forsooth! Not less than 15,000 people and 3,000 wagons had passed through Utah to the West before a Mormon ever set foot in Salt Lake Valley.

The road from Fort Bridger to this valley in 1847 was as plain as the road from Salt Lake City to Sandy is today. This I know, for I had traveled it prior to that time. General John Bidwell, now of Chico, California, and Captain Bartlett, of Jackson County, Missouri, went to California with an ox-train in 1841. Lansford W. Hastings and A.L. Lovejoy, both yet living, led a large party of wagon emigrants through to the Pacific Coast in 1842. In 1843 the regular annual overland emigration to Oregon and California began, and between that date and the time of the Mormon arrival in the valley in 1847, thousands had passed through Utah to the West; while the Saints are now boasting that "these valleys of the mountains" were discovered by the Lord to

the Prophet Brigham, who then by inspiration opened a "road to Utah," though that road had been regularly traveled for years.

The Saints neither discovered the country, nor built the roads, nor subdued the Indians: there was no such work to be done. The fact is, they entered into a beautiful, uninhabited, inviting and fertile valley. They were poor and isolated, and endured the ordinary hardships of their poverty and isolation. In that respect their condition and surroundings were far better than those of the early pioneers of the Mississippi Valley. And when we consider the advantages they have enjoyed, and their want of enterprise and energy, until the stream of progress from Gentile sources has forced them into a sort of unenviable notoriety . . . unenviable because of their opposition to the development of the Territory — the reactionary tendency and unAmerican character of their institutions becomes manifest.

Through the years many credible persons, such as J.R. McBride, have attempted to "set the record straight" concerning the claims of Mormon prophets. The historical sections of this book are included so that the reader may know of the true teachings of these prophets. Their importance exists in the immovable position of the Mormon Church and its leaders, that Mormon prophets, from Joseph Smith to today's president, are true revelators of God who are incapable of error in their statements and doctrine.

Contemporary officials make statements such as, "The Church is either true or it isn't. If it changes its stand on the strength of the great stream of modern religious and social thought, it will be proven untrue." (Paul C. Richards, Dialogue: *A Journal of Mormon Thought,* 1967, page 6).

Mormons believe that theirs is the only true church. They claim it was necessary to "restore the gospel," because all other churches are incomplete in that they do not have apostles and prophets. They believe in geneological work, baptizing for the dead, celestial marriage, also that the Bible is not a sufficient guide in itself and that their prophets receive latter day revelations. These beliefs are discussed herein.

A Mormon apostle George A. Smith declared, "If a faith will not bear to be investigated, if its preachers and professors are afraid to have it examined, their foundation must be very weak." *(Journal of Discourses,* v. 14, p. 216).

The quotations above, from the writings of respected Mormon apostles, not only endorse this investigation, but they actually encourage every Mormon to read them carefully. I am convinced that all who read will see clearly the discrepancies between the doctrines of Joseph Smith and the Holy Scriptures. It is my prayer that they will come, as I did, to faith in the one true Savior, Jesus Christ the Lord.

I

My God Was Too Small

If a faith will not bear to be investigated; if its preachers and professors are afraid to have it examined, their foundation must be very weak. – Journal of Discourses, Mormon Apostle George A. Smith, v. 14, p. 216.

This quotation puts the stamp of approval of the Mormon Church upon all those who examine the foundations of this popular movement. Such a book as this should be read by all those interested in Mormonism and by the members of that church.

Here the discrepancies between the teachings of Joseph Smith and those of the Bible can be clearly seen.

I grew up in the Mormon faith in Utah and was taught, as thousands of others have been, that the Church of Jesus Christ of Latter Day Saints (Mormon) is the "True Church." All other denominations, we learned, were guilty of apostasy, as Joseph Smith said, "an abomination" in God's sight. (*The Pearl of Great Price,* 1943 ed., p. 48) According to my instructors, eternal salvation depended on baptism and obedience to the ordinances and discipline of our church, and upon a life of good works.

Under the teachings of the Mormon Church, "God himself was once as we are now, and is an exalted man. . . .All you have got to learn is how to be gods yourselves, the same as all gods have done before you." (*Journal of Discourses,* Vol. I, p. 50)

As a young man, this teaching disturbed me more and more. It was a dual burden to my youthful idealism that my God and Creator was only an exalted man and that I must attain to being a god. I did not feel godlike. I was bitterly inadequate for such an assignment. But more persistent than this was the longing for a God who was greater than any man. It is popular today to call Mormonism the "religion of young men." How many of these young Latter Day Saints realize as I did that they fail in godliness, and yearn for a God Who is not at all like any man, a God Who has never been like any man?

In my youthful restlessness I came to California and there I met a fine Catholic girl. Soon I loved her deeply and I did not allow the difference in our religions to trouble me. I was still convinced that the Church of Jesus Christ of Latter Day Saints was the only true church, and so I asked permission from my Bishop to marry out of our faith. I received his blessing, with the understanding that we would all try to convert my wife to Mormonism.

Although we shared a great love for one another, we also shared a sense of emptiness in our lives. Regardless of the happiness of our marriage, we realized that there was something missing from our activities. We went to worldly amusements which failed to amuse, tried many pleasures which did not please. I asked my wife, "What is it all about? Isn't there more to life than this?"

She suggested that we attend church together and was willing to attend the Mormon Church and to take instruction from two Mormon missionary ladies.

My brother William, who had followed me to California, had begun to read the Bible. The Holy Spirit, with no human instrument, had brought him to a saving knowledge of Christ through the written Word. At his prompting I read a Christian magazine in which, for the first time, I read a message concerning the new birth.

God was moving in people and circumstances around me. A man who was employed by me told me that he had accepted Christ and had been saved. I questioned him about his presumption in saying that he was saved, for I had been taught that no one could be "saved" until the great Day of Judgment. He suggested that I attend meetings being held nearby by the "Crew of the Good Ship Grace."

On the night of the meeting we decided we would go, but when we arrived, the church was so full we had to sit on the platform, with other latecomers. Sitting so close to the speakers, as I listened I was convinced of their sincerity and the reality of the assurance they possessed. Even the music thrilled me and the message of Truth led me to accept Christ as Savior that night.

As the Mormon missionaries were coming to complete my wife's instruction, preceding her being baptized, I realized there were many things which we must have settled. We turned for counseling to an evangelist who was in the city. When I went in my car to bring him to our home, I surely did not expect the Mormon missionaries to be there upon my return. I had invited them to come but they had said they doubted they would be able, and so I did not mention them to our visitor. When my wife opened the door of our home, to my surprise I found the room filled with Mormon people. Before I could make any explanation, immediately after the introductions, the evangelist began to speak, "Brother Anderson has asked me about the Mormon Church, and I want to explain it to him."

Through my embarrassment and confusion I was amazed to hear the Mormons question him, "Where do you get your authority?" "Have you read the *Book of Mormon*?" At every point of Scripture he gave they interrupted with many questions.

Of course by this time he realized that they were Mormons, but during the discussion many of the questions that had been troubling me had been resolved. My guest made no disparaging remarks about the Mormon Church, but proved clearly that no church could save; only Christ alone. God was marvelously using this unusual situation to clarify for me and my wife His great plan of salvation. When I told them all that I had heard enough to be convinced that Mormonism was in error, we brought the meeting to a close.

Our evangelist friend left with us a tract by Dr. H. A. Ironside, the late pastor of the Moody Memorial Church, which compared the Mormon beliefs with the Word of God. Through it, the glorious simplicity of Titus 3:5 was born anew in my heart, *"Not by works of righteousness which we have done, but according to His mercy He saved us."*

At last I could stop trying, and trust. Just a few days before my wife was to have been baptized into the Mormon Church she too accepted Jesus Christ as Savior. For us, Ephesians 2:8 and 9 made all things clear, *"For by grace are ye saved through faith; and that not of yourselves; it is the gift of God: not of works, lest any man should boast."*

My God was great enough!

II

A Missionary Venture

Mormonism is now an organization with a root system so expansive and so well entrenched that every day a new Mormon chapel is dedicated, somewhere in the world. The church claims more than three million members worldwide, and more than two million in the United States, and has indoctrination classes for youths and adults.

In spite of all this, I was convinced that not only did few non-Mormons understand the Mormon faith, but that few Mormons really had grasped the simple clarity of the message of Christ. As I began to study the Bible I took courage to witness to some of my family and Mormon friends about the saving knowledge of our Lord.

I would lie awake at night thinking of friends with whom I had attended school in Utah. I was convinced that if I could go back and explain the gospel to them some would believe. I had an undeniable desire to return to my birthplace in Utah and tell others of the peace and joy in Christ.

Three years after I became a Christian, the way was opened for me to make my first "missionary journey" into Utah with Mr. Krist Gudnason, who, like my parents, had been born in Iceland. This fine Christian businessman and worker in the Gideon Society of California could, I felt sure, reach many of our Icelandic people in Utah who had become Mormons.

Eagerly I wrote ahead to a family friend, Ole Olson, asking if some of our friends would meet in his home with Mr. Gudnason and me. I explained that Mr. Gudnason had recently returned from Iceland, that he could show pictures of his trip and I suggested that we could sing hymns and read the Bible together. A letter came saying that he knew I had left the Mormon Church and that he was eager to cooperate with us and wished to talk with me.

When we arrived in my home town of Spanish Fork and went to call on Mr. Olson, I was amazed to be met at the door by Ole Olson standing there in total silence.

16

"Mr. Olson, do you know me?" I asked.

His reply was simple, "I know who you are."

I realized then what had happened—some of our Mormon friends, hearing about the plans for a meeting, had brought pressure upon Mr. Olson to stop such a meeting. As I feared, he informed me that the plans were cancelled. Without any opportunity to introduce my companion, Mr. Gudnason, I simply told Mr. Olson that I would see him the next day. Needless to say, we went away somewhat distressed.

Next we called upon my cousin, then a social worker for the Welfare Department of Utah, but when she came to the door she said, "Einar, you must leave your religion outside. Your friends like you but they don't want anything to do with your new religion."

You can imagine my amazement, for although I had not seen her for four years, she did not ask me in nor acknowledge the presence of my companion.

That night in my room I asked the Lord the meaning of all that had happened that day, and asked what He would have us do next. The Scripture I Peter 4:12-14 was brought to my mind:

> *Beloved, think it not strange concerning the fiery trial which is to try you, as though some strange thing happened unto you:*
>
> *But rejoice, inasmuch as ye are partakers of Christ's sufferings; that, when his glory shall be revealed, ye may be glad also with exceeding joy.*
>
> *If ye be reproached for the name of Christ, happy are ye; for the spirit of glory and of God resteth upon you:*

I then humbly realized that we were being rejected for Christ's sake.

First thing the next morning, I received a letter from my wife in which she quoted at the close this Scripture:

> *But as we were allowed of God to be put in trust with the gospel, even so we speak; not as pleasing men, but God, which trieth our hearts.* (I Thessalonians 2:4)

These were the words of encouragement I had needed. Previously we had felt the Lord had been leading us to Utah; now, in the face of closed doors, I had received assurance from God's Word that He would have us stay. Mr. Gudnason agreed and we simply laid our plans in the Lord's hands. Then we went out to call on some acquaintances I had known.

We stopped at the Spanish Fork High School and I found the principal whom I had known when I attended there. He introduced us to the professors of the seminary and when they learned that Mr. Gudnason was the President of the Gideon Society of California they informed us that they were about to send for fifteen new Bibles from the American Bible Society, to be used in their classes. We were delighted to tell them that we had in our car Gideon Bibles which we would donate for that purpose. Here again the provision of the Lord was evident for He had led us to bring these Bibles. When they offered to pay for the Bibles we were glad to explain that these Bibles had been paid for by Christians for such a ministry, but we requested the privilege of presenting them to the student body. One of the two professors seemed reluctant to grant this request, but we were allowed five minutes for our presentation. During this time, after Mr. Gudnason had explained how he, as a book salesman, was won to Christ by a hotel keeper in Denmark and that his life had changed, and after I had said a few words, we were permitted to continue, by vote of the class.

After we spoke, many young people came to us for questions. It was evident that these Mormon youths were hungry for the simple words of salvation, so familiar to us.

From this experience we realized that the Lord was working and that we must proceed, moment by moment, totally under the guidance of the Holy Spirit.

The next day, driving on the highway, I noticed several boys walking down the road, indicating that they wished a ride. As we approached them I exclaimed, "Mr. Gudnason, those boys were in yesterday's meeting at the seminary."

We gave them a ride and mentioned our plans to make moving pictures of the Iceland monument which had been erected. One of the boys explained that he had had some experience in photography and asked if he could help. Then the others wanted to come along, so we agreed to meet them on the following morning, providing their parents approved.

Before they arrived at our motel the next day we had prayed for these boys, asking the Lord to lead our conversation and make our witness effective. It was therefore no surprise to us when one of the boys asked, "Mr. Anderson, what is wrong with Mormonism?"

Until this moment we had not mentioned Mormonism to the boys, but they evidently had heard that I had recently left the Mormon faith.

Remembering the verse in I Thessalonians, I could only reply, "You have asked a good question, and I want to give you the answer."

I explained to them that though I had been a Mormon all my life it was not until I heard the gospel later in California that I realized it was Christ alone Who could save me. We asked them to sit down and read God's plan of salvation from the Bible.

After answering their questions and showing them by the Scriptures how they could be saved by faith in Christ, we asked them if they wished to receive Him as their Savior, and upon their assent we knelt in prayer as all five of those boys made sincere professions of faith in Christ.

In the meantime, other boys and girls who had attended the seminary Bible presentation had returned to their homes and told of Einar Anderson and Krist Gudnason speaking at their school. According to His glorious power God was working.

Ole Olson, who had rejected us, now contacted us to say that he had heard about the seminary experience and would like us to proceed with our original arrangements. Thus we did meet in his home, as previously planned. Mr. Gudnason spoke and showed the pictures of his recent trip to Iceland to the friends gathered there and the testimony and message that I gave was again honored. At the close of the evening Mr. Gudnason and Ole Olson, with arms around each other, sang in Icelandic, the wonderful hymn, "What a Friend we Have in Jesus."

Can you imagine our gratitude for the doors God was opening? During the few days we spent in Spanish Fork, many individuals came to understand the love of God and His gift of salvation through Christ.

As in the case of one lady employed in a dress shop, they would say to us, "All my life I have wanted to make a comparison between Mormonism and some other religion." And thus the opportunity would be made for us to read to them Romans 4:1-5, closing with those glorious words, *"But to him that worketh not, but believeth on him that justifieth the ungodly, his faith is counted for righteousness."*

Anyone brought up in the traditional Christian faith cannot realize the miracle these words seem to those taught from childhood such erroneous beliefs as this:

> Once we have been resurrected, it will be our own efforts, and not Christ's sacrifice, that will be the deciding factor. (Bennet, Wallace, *Why I Am a Mormon*, N.Y., 1958, p. 191)

Or the following statements, which contradict God's plan of salvation:

> The full benefit of the atonement, however, comes to us only upon condition of our obedience to the gospel plan. We must accept this plan and comply with its ordinances by "performing the symbols which stand for its reality." (Brown, Hugh B., *Eternal Quest*, Salt Lake, 1958, p. 414)
>
> A man can be saved only so fast as he gains knowledge of the laws of God. This law of eternal progression is symbolized by a learning process during the endowment and without mastery of which the recipient cannot advance. Salvation is obtained by obedi-

ence to the laws upon which such blessings are predicated. (Berrett, William Edwin, *The Restored Church*, Salt Lake, 1937, p. 520)

This Mormon teaching that a man can be saved only as fast as he gains knowledge of the laws of God is nullified by the teachings of the Word of God:

"For after that in the wisdom of God the world by wisdom knew not God, it pleased God by the foolishness of preaching to save them that believe."—I Cor. 1:21. It pleased God to "save them that believe."

No wonder the dear Mormon people cried out to us, "I can understand salvation for the first time in my life," when they are shown John 1:12, *"But as many as received him, to them gave he power to become the sons of God, even to them that believe on his name."*

On this missionary venture into Utah we often heard men or women say to us, "The Bible has become a new book for me." God had wonderfully answered our prayers. I realized that the Lord was showing me a path of service. The burden of confusion I had experienced as a youthful Mormon could be lifted from other heavy hearts. Without personal experience as a Mormon, or without a thorough understanding of the Mormon religion, its history and its deviations from traditional Christianity, it would be difficult to convince Mormons of our complete salvation through the Lord Jesus Christ.

This is the reason we deal with these matters here, so that both Mormons and non—Mormons can have a better understanding of the LDS organization, charged with converting the world.

III

Mormon Beginnings

To understand Mormon doctrines, and how they affect the lives of their adherents, we must give some thought to the men who "received" those doctrines and "revealed" them to their followers.

The Mormon story, as told to the world by the church's missionaries, is briefly this:

In the third or fourth century after Christ, the world rejected the message of His twelve apostles. The world then went into apostasy, fell into spiritual decay, and there was not even a shadow of its presence to be seen upon the earth. Christ's teachings were perverted, ordinances were changed, and there was no inspired prophet. Therefore, God's ordinances could not be administered acceptably to God, and mankind was left to wander in spiritual darkness. Joseph Smith was chosen by God to restore the church once again to this earth. Therefore, in 1820 the Lord revealed Himself to Joseph Smith, in answer to his prayer. God the Father and His Son appeared and told Smith to join none of the churches for they and their creeds were "an abomination in the sight of God." A few years later, the angel Moroni appeared to Joseph Smith and called him by name, stating that God had work for him to do. Moroni said there was a "deposited" book, written upon golden plates, giving an account of the inhabitants of this earth, and containing the fulness of the everlasting gospel, as delivered by the Savior to the ancient inhabitants.

Smith's story of the translation of this book (the *Book of Mormon* which is equal in the eyes of the Mormons to the Bible) requires of his followers considerable credulity.

THE STORY ACCORDING TO JOSEPH SMITH

The angel had told Joseph that there were two stones in silver bows which, when fastened to a breastplate, constituted the *Urim* and *Thummin*. Possessing these stones, Joseph would be able to translate the book. The Angel Moroni appeared three times that night, and on

21

other occasions, to Joseph Smith and warned that the plates and the seer-stone spectacles (Urim and Thummin) must only be shown to those to whom the Lord would command that they be revealed. In a vision Joseph could see the place where the plates were hidden, and subsequently he found them, near his home, in Ontario County, New York, on the west side of a hill, under a stone of considerable size, deposited in a stone box. There he also found the Urim and Thummin, as had been promised in his vision.

Later, to the *Book of Mormon* (which had come into existence in such a mysterious manner) there were added other sacred revelations, the *Doctrine and Covenants* and the *Pearl of Great Price*. Upon these and upon more recent revelations to "Latter Day Saints" are based the doctrines and tenets of the Mormon faith.

A Mormon must believe that Joseph Smith was the Prophet, Seer, and Revelator—the means through which the true Gospel was restored to earth. They call their religion "the Restored Gospel."

Thus, the Mormons received their Moses—Joseph Smith, and their Bible—the *Book of Mormon*, for three years after the "plates" were discovered Joseph Smith founded the Church of Jesus Christ of Latter Day Saints, which grew from a small number of Smith's neighbors and relatives, to nearly one hundred thousand followers by the time of his death.

To comprehend the zeal of these forceful people and their allegiance to their church, one must understand the men who were their leaders.

JOSEPH SMITH, JR. – NO MIDDLE GROUND

Latter Day leader, Prophet and Apostle Joseph Fielding Smith, declared this requirement of faith for Mormons, "Mormonism, as it is called, must stand or fall on the story of Joseph Smith. He was either a prophet of God, divinely called, properly appointed and commissioned, or he was one of the biggest frauds this world has ever seen. There is no middle ground." (Smith, Joseph Fielding, *Doctrines of Salvation*, p. 188)

We submit, for your own judgment, the basic, historical facts about the life of Joseph Smith. He was born in Sharon, Vermont, December 23, 1805, the fourth child of Lucy and Joseph Smith. The senior Smith was known to spend most of his time digging for imaginary treasures. At one time he was involved in litigation after trying to mint his own currency. Joseph, like his father, was a dreamer and visionary. Documents are available which show that young Joseph was brought before

Currency minted by Joseph Smith

the court of the State of New York as a "Glass looker," in 1826. He confessed that he had a certain stone used to determine where hidden or lost treasures were, and that for a price he had told where gold mines were, but claimed that though this had been his habit for three years he had "pretty much given it up" on account of "his health," and that he did not solicit such business.

Lucy Smith once testified that her son participated in and supervised treasure-digging expeditions, but after he became famous she denied this. She had said that her son was a "peek stone" addict. The young "prophet" would place a stone in his hat, put his face into the hat and then see into the stone to determine by its deep mysteries where certain treasures lay. Young Smith had romantic interests also and eventually eloped with Emma Hale, whose father despised what Smith stood for and would not sanction the marriage.

According to the sworn testimony of a one-time neighbor and friend of young Smith, given seven months after his elopement with Emma Hale, a confrontation took place between Joseph and Emma's father, in Harmony, Pennsylvania. The neighbor, named Ingersol, testified on January 18, 1827:

> His [Joseph Smith's] father-in-law addressed Joseph in a flood of tears: "You have stolen my daughter and married her. I had much rather have followed her to her grave. You spend your time in digging for money—pretend to see in a stone and thus try to deceive people." Joseph wept and acknowledged that he could not see in a stone now nor ever could, that his former pretensions in that respect were false. He then promised to give up his old habits and digging for money and looking into stones. . . .(Howe, E. D., *Mormonism Unveiled*, Zanesville, Ohio, 1834, p. 234)

This admission by Joseph Smith to his father-in-law was never denied. The prophet's promise to abandon his visions and spells and diggings was soon broken, for, according to history, on September 21, 1827, Joseph made what he later said was his fourth annual ascent of the Hill of Cumorah. Here this intense young man declared he received the plates which (whether this was his intention at the time or not) became the *Book of Mormon*. The plates were written in "Reformed Egyptian" by Mormon, the father of the Angel Moroni, claimed Smith, and contained the extensive history of how Jesus Christ, after the crucifixion and resurrection, appeared on the American continent. When published as the *Book of Mormon* these revelations covered religious and political concepts couched in Biblical language imitating the King James translation.

Extensive source material studied by this writer regarding the true authorship of the *Book of Mormon* reveals the Spaulding story as most plausible. Authenticated by affidavits and newspaper and other documentation we read that Solomon Spaulding wrote a novel, attempting to account for the American Indian by Israelitish origin and this piece of fiction was later re-written by Spaulding into a story called "Manuscript Found." (The first outline for it is at Oberlin College.) The story was left with a publisher, from whom it was stolen under circumstances which led the author to suspect Joseph Smith's close friend and confederate Sidney Rigdon. It is claimed that the historical portions of "Manuscript Found" and the *Book of Mormon* are the same, and that the religious teachings are interjected in the King James phraseology of the Bible. The debate as to whether the *Book of Mormon* is plagiarism of the Spaulding novel will no doubt continue through the years.

One thing is clear, that however the 300,000 word *Book of Mormon* came into being, without it the uneducated, unambitious farm boy would not have blossomed into the self-assured promoter of a new religion in so short a time.

In 1831, a year after the organization of his church, young Joseph, his bride and a few disciples moved to Kirtland, Ohio, and soon two thousand converts were added. During the next thirteen years, Smith is reported to have received 135 direct revelations from God. One of these revealed that Christ, on His return, would establish the land of Zion in America.

Joseph Smith went to Missouri to scout the exact location of the "Promised Land." On August 3, 1831, on a high promontory in Jackson County, Missouri, 63 acres of "holy ground" were chosen for the Temple of Zion, to be Christ's earthly headquarters. But soon after the saints relocated in this spot they were driven from Jackson County at gun point.

They moved to the state of Illinois, where they built a politically oriented city, the Mormon town of Nauvoo, which became the largest city in the state, and their number increased to five thousand.

One of the prophet's revelations, however, caused sorrow and bloodshed. This was the Polygamy Revelation which the Latter Day Saints wish to be considered a dead issue. When pressed into conversation regarding "plural marriages," Mormon missionaries defend the doctrine, although in 1890, to comply with Federal law their president's "Manifesto" advised the Mormons to discontinue the practice.

Joseph Smith, in a moment of insight, expressed the premonition that this doctrine could be their ruin. An interview with William Marks,

Mormon Temple at Nauvoo, Illionis.

reported in *Zion's Harbinger* and *Baneemy's Organ*, Vol. III (July 1853), pp. 52, 53, tells of Joseph saying:

> We are a ruined people.
> This doctrine of polygamy, or spiritual wife-system, that has been taught and practiced among us, will prove our destruction and overthrow. I have been deceived; it is a curse to mankind, and we shall have to leave the United States soon, unless it can be put down, and its practice stopped in the Church.

The prophet sought a way out of his predicament too late. During the early 1840s polygamy had been practiced secretly by the Mormon leaders. William Law, a disenchanted follower of Smith, started a newspaper, the Nauvoo *Expositor*, which revealed this fact to the unknowing saints. Soon sensual stories were circulated and the world at large began to attack this practice of the Mormons.

Joseph Smith had reached the zenith of his influence. Membership in his church stood at 100,000. He enjoyed his large personal fortune, his position as mayor of Nauvoo, his own militia, and he had even announced his candidacy for the Presidency of the United States. His political power was declared to be equal to that of the state government.

Human power corrupts. Dissensions began among the faithful. The storm broke when the Mormon armed guard, called the *Legion of Nauvoo*, on orders from its leaders, went to the Nauvoo *Expositor* office, pied the type and burned every issue of the paper on hand.

Governor Ford learned of the burning and destruction of the newspaper by the Mormons. He wrote to the prophet demanding that he and everyone implicated in these unlawful acts toward the *Expositor* "submit immediately to the Carthage constable and come to the city for trial." The Governor was quoted as saying that he would "call out the militia if necessary to bring the offenders to justice."

Now the Prophet-General-Mayor must submit to the law or flee. He called a meeting of the Mormon leaders at the Mansion House. That night Smith and his brother Hyrum, with a few of their closest associates escaped, but returned soon, only to find orders from Governor Ford which required the Legion of Nauvoo to surrender all their

Joseph Smith, Jr.—the Mormon prophet

"Lieutenant-General" Joseph Smith reviewing the Nauvoo Legion.

Jail at Carthage, Illinois

weapons; Smith countersigned the order and proceeded on horseback with his brother and friends to go to Carthage to surrender.

At Carthage the town was in a wild uproar, many demanding to see the "prophet." The Governor of Illinois himself came to Carthage and had long debates with Smith at the jail. Joseph had felt that he was going to his death in Carthage, where indeed tension grew, both inside and outside the jail. Finally a mob broke into the jail, shooting Joseph's brother Hyrum first, wounding Mormon John Taylor, and at last, as the prophet attempted to escape through the window, shooting Joseph Smith.

The tragic murders, that hot Thursday afternoon of June 27, 1844, may have welded the Mormons together in their grief. The death of their leader did not mean the death of Mormonism. The prophet's followers mourned their leader as a martyr, which was not literally true. A martyr, according to English dictionaries, is one who suffers death as a penalty of witnessing to and refusing to renounce his religion or the principles and practice thereof. Joseph Smith and his co-conspirators were jailed for breaking the law, and even in jail were armed with guns and attempted to defend themselves, until they were outnumbered. In Mormon writings, this fact is never found. Eminent biographer Irving Wallace, in his book *The Twenty-seventh Wife,* describes the scene in the Carthage jail, stating that Smith snatched a six-barrel pistol when the attackers forced the cell door, shot at the mobsters, wounding three of them. But their volley had caught Hyrum, killing him instantly. "With odds insurmountable, Smith threw down his pistol and leaped for the window. As he ascended the ledge, bullets exploding through the smoking cell door and from the court below struck him."

Mormon writers go so far as to compare Smith's death with that of Jesus Christ, saying, "Christ sealed His testimony with His blood on Calvary—Joseph Smith sealed his testimony with his blood at Carthage, Illinois." (Weber Stake Ward Teacher's Lesson for Jan., 1922, an L.D.S. Publication)

At Joseph Smith's birthplace in Vermont, which has been called by Mormons the "Bethlehem of Mormonism," is the "the World's Largest Polished Shaft," a memorial to the prophet. He created a book and a religion—a religion that told men they could be gods themselves. Perhaps the best epitaph written for him was this, "Since power was sweet to him, he gave to every convert the promise of dominion over a star."

Death of Joseph Smith.

IV

Utah— The Promised Land

When Joseph and Hyrum Smith were killed, Brigham Young was the president of the Twelve Apostles and on the day of the shooting happened to be in Boston on business for the church. He quickly returned and used every cunning means to assume the leadership of Joseph's flock. He proved to be one of the greatest promoters and colonizers in American history.

A number of Joseph's followers refused to accept Brigham Young as head of the church, choosing, in 1860, the son of Joseph Smith the prophet as their leader. This group, with the exception of the Utah Mormons, of course, is the largest of the many branches of Mormonism and is called the Reorganized Church of Jesus Christ of Latter Day Saints. They follow the "original teachings and commandments of God," and deny that polygamy was ever taught or practiced by Joseph Smith. This group still believes that the "gathering to Zion," before Christ's return, will take place in Missouri, where their headquarters are located at Independence.

Within Mormonism are several other factions, all claiming to be the "true Mormon Church." They staunchly believe that Joseph Smith was the prophet of God and that the *Book of Mormon* is the Word of God. We will not include here all the laborious details of the differences in doctrine of these various factions, but to name a few, there are:

The Church of Christ (Temple Lot), which had 3,000 members in 12 churches in 1956, and was founded at Bloomington, Illinois at the time of Joseph Smith's death. This group returned to Independence, Missouri in 1867 and began raising funds for the purchase of a temple lot upon which to erect the temple of the Lord for the day of His return and the gathering of the ten lost tribes of Israel. (The lot was to be the center of the New Jerusalem, but was lost to the Reorganized Church in a lawsuit in 1891-95.) This dissenting body rejected the teachings of baptism for the dead, the elevation of men to the estate of gods following death, the doctrine of lineal right to office in the church, and the practice of polygamy.

31

The Church of Jesus Christ (Bickertonites), organized in 1862, under the leadership of Sidney Rigdon, . . . whose followers also condemned the teaching of polygamy and plurality of gods and baptism for the dead. The last report available was of 2,346 members and 46 churches.

The Church of Jesus Christ (Cutlerites) organized in 1853 with one congregation in Independence, Missouri, and the other at Clitherall, Minnesota.

The Church of Jesus Christ (Strangites) whose founder, James J. Strang, was crowned "king" of his church in 1850 and was murdered in 1856 during a wave of anti-Mormonism in the Great Lakes area. Organized at Burlington, Wisconsin, in 1844, this church denied the virgin birth and the atonement.

The Church of the Firstborn of the Fulness of Times, perhaps the best known of the "Fundamentalist" groups of Mormons which practice polygamy openly today, is located in Colorado City, Arizona.

The churches above listed are recorded by the U.S. Department of Commerce and the National Council of Churches, with the exception of the Church of the Firstborn of the Fulness of Times.

Old Salt Lake Theatre (left) and East First South Street as it looked in 1869. In this historic building Porter Rockwell attended a theatrical performance on the evening of his death.

**Entrance to Mormon Church (Strangite)
Burlington, Wisconsin.**

BRIGHAM'S BAND

If it can be said that the Utah Mormons would never have arrived at their present vast organization without the leadership of Brigham Young, it can also be said that Brigham Young could never have succeeded so astonishingly without the staunch perseverance of those early Mormon pioneers.

Brigham Young avoided the mistakes that brought his predecessor to ruin. He proposed to take his people apart from the society into which their doctrines could not fit. He skillfully set about to harness his empire building qualities and to fire the imagination of hardy zealots, inspired by Joseph Smith's visions. These pioneers believed that men can become as God, and they worked tirelessly, even magnificently, to accomplish their global goals.

This vigorous leader, who had stepped in to succeed Prophet Smith, announced to the Mormons of Nauvoo that he would lead them to a "promised land."

Hard-headed, strong and self-willed, "Briggie," as he was called,

**Statue of Brigham Young in the foreground. Mormon
Temple in the background.**

possessed great charm and ample leadership abilities. Young did not see
visions or dream dreams. He was a practical opportunist, and by 1846
he had organized a mass exodus that was to lead the Latter Day Saints
to the Wasatch Mountains at Utah's Great Salt Lake, where the Mormons began to make the desert blossom and produce.

In one year, it is told that 450 houses were built for a population of
5,000. Within ten years 135 Mormon communities were built, with a
total population of 76,335 in Idaho, Wyoming, New Mexico and
California. When Brigham Young died, in 1877, there had been 360
towns built in which there were 140,000 people. Brigham Young
presided over every enterprise. This portly and courtly man presided
over a church, railroads, telegraph, newspaper, manufacturing and retail
enterprises, as well as the vast farming undertakings.

In Utah the Mormons had a self-governing community, and in 1850,
by act of Congress, Utah Territory was organized, with Brigham Young
as governor. Joseph Smith and Brigham Young had much in common;
one quality was their ability to turn misfortune into opportunity. If

Brigham Young was more fearless and ruthless, he was no less daring. Regardless of the troubles that polygamy had brought to the Mormons, he not only ordained that it should continue but practiced it as some have said "magnificently." Furthermore, he gave new scope to the church's missionary ventures, baptism for the dead, marriage for eternity and all the secret temple practices that Smith had received in revelations. Before we discuss the other doctrines and tenets of the Mormon faith we will examine those probably best known but little understood practices of the Church of Jesus Christ of Latter Day Saints. It is because of many of these practices that Mormons have never been understood.

POLYGAMY YESTERDAY

The importance of Joseph Smith's polygamy revelation is such that it is not possible to properly evaluate the doctrines of this church without studying this teaching. To the mind casually acquainted with Mormonism, polygamy is always associated with the sect. The connection between this belief and the whole structure of their church doctrine is undeniable.

The fact that in 1890 it was necessary (in order to secure statehood) for their President Wilford Woodruff to publish a manifesto declaring, "my advice to the Latter Day Saints is to refrain from contracting any marriage forbidden by the law of the land," has not changed Mormon belief in this revelation.

The Mormons who practice polygamy do so because they believe it was a divine mandate of Joseph Smith, an "everlasting covenant" irreversible, sanctioned and fortified by Brigham Young and other leaders. Joseph Fielding Smith admitted in 1942 that the position of the United States Government regarding the Mormon practice of polygamy was an "affliction" to the "saints." He wrote (*Essentials in Church History*, p. 606) that the Latter Day Saints felt the anti-polygamy legislation a restriction of their religious rights. When the Supreme Court sustained these laws, the church was forced to submit but they never felt it was within their power to suspend a "commandment given to them by revelation from the Lord."

Mormons are told officially that the "crowning gospel ordinance requisite for Godhood is celestial marriage." They believe in a "heavenly Father and Heavenly Mother," and they believe their laws which state that if they obey this "holy ordinance and all other principles of the Gospel," they shall "be Gods."

Heady, as well as sensually and spiritually exciting as the "patriarchal order of marriage" was, Joseph Smith at first kept the revelation for only a few of his closest friends, not desiring to give "strong meat" to those of the group unprepared for such blessings. Brigham Young's problems were different from those of Smith. Young was proud to claim that the "result of our endless union would be offspring as numerous as the stars of heaven, or the sands of the seashore." He had a frontier to conquer.

On August 29, 1852, Young announced in the tabernacle that a "revelation on Plural Marriage" had been made to the prophet Joseph Smith, at Nauvoo, and there written by him, July 12, 1843. One of the covenants in this respect, entered into and sealed by the Mormon priesthood, was that if a man were endowed with "keys of the power," then "if he do anything in my name and according to my law, and by my word, he will not commit sin, and I will justify him." (*Doctrine and Covenants* 132:59)

Brigham Young, "on that day in 1852 when he introduced the polygamy doctrine publicly, was, according to Utah biographers, the husband of twenty women." (*Differences that Persist,* Reorganized Church of Jesus Christ of Latter Day Saints, Missouri, 1959, p. 16) The number of his wives greatly increased after that date.

As the leaders went, so went the followers. There is abundant evidence to prove that early Mormons not only practiced polygamy but were all but forced to do so—they were "encouraged" by violent and vicious means. The violence, to be described in the following chapter, went hand-in-hand with the increase in immorality of the Mormon people during their years of public polygamy. They were in their own Promised Land and they could live free from the "corrupting" influence of the Gentiles (as they called all non-Mormons). *The Millenial Star* (Mormon newspaper) once reported that a man with forty wives might have 3,508,441 descendants by the time he was seventy-eight years old. Among the alleged forty-five wives of Mormon President Heber C. Kimball there were four sets of sisters.

The plural marriage doctrine, as set forth by Joseph Smith is, in part:

> And again as pertaining to the law of the Priesthood: If any man espouse a virgin, and desire to espouse another, and the first give her consent; and if he espouse the second, and they are virgins, and have vowed to no other man, then is he justified; he cannot commit adultery; for they are given unto him; for he cannot commit adultery with that that belongeth unto him and to no one else; and if he have ten virgins given unto him by this law, he cannot commit adultery, for they belong to him, and they are given unto him, therefore is he justified. But if one of either of the ten virgins,

after she is espoused, shall be with another man, she has committed adultery, and shall be destroyed; for they are given unto him to multiply and replenish the earth, according to my commandment, and to fulfill the promise which was given by my Father before the foundation of the world and for their exaltation in the eternal worlds, that they may bear the souls of men; for herein is the work of my Father continued, that He may be glorified. (*Doctrine and Covenants* Section 132:4, 59, 61-63; 1944 edition)

The Mormons claim that at the death of Brigham Young there was "rejoicing among the enemies of the Church, who thought it was due to his strong personality and force of character that 'Mormonism' endured." They could not realize that if there was rejoicing it was that the most outstanding exponent of polygamy in the world had left the scene of religious prominence. There runs through the communities of the Church of Jesus Christ of Latter Day Saints a strong sense of persecution, which no doubt dates back to the days when Smith and his followers were driven out of their homes because of the immoral practices of many of their leaders.

President John Taylor, who succeeded Brigham Young, found that he could not successfully hold back the opposition to the practice of polygamy. Mormons themselves agree that during this period the Protestant churches and "nearly every paper in the United States" bitterly denounced the practice of plural marriage.

In 1879, President Hayes sent out a circular letter through the office of the Secretary of State to the diplomatic officers of the United States in foreign countries, advising them that large numbers of persons from various lands were coming to the United States for the purpose of joining the Mormons in Utah, and stating that the marriage system of the Mormons was a crime against the statutes of the country. These immigrants, he said, came "to swell the numbers of the law-defying Mormons of Utah."

It was the Edmunds Bill which became law in 1882 which made punishable the contracting of plural marriage, as well as polygamous living. The Mormon President Taylor went into exile, with his counselors, and there he died. Again the Mormons cried "martyr" and condemned the United States Government.

POLYGAMY TODAY

Now the federal law could be enforced and many Mormon men were jailed for lewd cohabitation. By June, 1887, approximately 200 were in jail. The Edmunds-Tucker Act had dissolved the Corporation of the Church of Jesus Christ of Latter Day Saints, which destroyed that political and economic institution. To solve their problems the Mormon settlements would have to become a state.

By this time, Wilford Woodruff was the President of the church and in 1890 he showed *The Manifesto* to a prominent LDS member who had connections with the President of the United States, hoping this would solve the pressures upon his people. It was made public on September 24, 1890, and appears at the very end of the *Doctrine and Covenants*.

The Mormons were faced with a dilemma. Their problem was this: having taught, approved and encouraged polygamy officially for many years, in accordance with their *Doctrine and Covenants* Section 132, they found it profitable and necessary to rescind this doctrine.

The "spiritual importance" of plural marriage was among the many revelations of Joseph Smith and practiced by him. Then their great leader Brigham Young not only sanctioned polygamy but set the example by his many marriages (he was rumored to have had at least 27, perhaps more, wives). The large families were felt to be a necessity for practical reasons of the labor required to build the great Salt Lake establishment into practically an autonomous nation. The promised spiritual advantages were also great and wives who complained were reminded that the martyr's crown would be theirs and great would be the reward in heaven. And so some would spin, others weave cloth for clothing the large families as well as attending the cattle and helping with irrigation and farm chores. "Children were everywhere. 'Babies seem indigenous to Salt Lake,' " was a quotation given in Stanley P. Hirshon's Biography of Brigham Young. (*The Lion of the Lord,* p. 134)

Then, when the frontier had been conquered, and Utah was eager for statehood and peace, the strategic move was to repeal the church's approval of polygamy, even under a threat of excommunication.

Polygamy, nevertheless, has been very hard to stamp out. The reason is a religious one. The church had tampered with one of its fundamental institutions. Although Woodruff said that his Manifesto was the result of a revelation, the saints had to decide whose revelations to believe—Young's and Smith's or Woodruff's. Polygamy has sprung up again and again in Mormon circles and has always existed. Those who take the Holy Books of Mormonism literally ask, "If God ordains plural marriage and the Prophet Joseph put it in the *Doctrine and Covenants,* how can man change it?" There is logic in their position, and yet they are forced to live outside the law or admit that their church is governed by man-made laws and man-given promises.

Today Mormon polygamists surreptitiously practice their unnatural unions and are puzzled by the inconsistency of present leaders who discourage this practice. When they are arrested and charged with "unlawful cohabitation," they declare simply that in the sight of God they are properly married, according to their church's doctrines. These curious cases seldom come to trial. The Latter Day Saints do not care to have Section 132 of their *Doctrine and Covenants* publicized, nor do they wish to have their esteemed founders quoted on this subject. Consequently, many polygamists today live in Salt Lake, and in other cities with large Mormon populations, undisturbed by legal action.

"If it is true at all," the polygamists claim, "it is *all* true!" Brigham taught clearly, "The only men who become Gods, even the sons of God, are those who enter through polygamy." It is understandable, therefore, that there are an estimated seventy thousand faithful Mormons today who consider themselves to be "fundamentalists" among those who practice the written Mormon law, but who are an embarrassment to the modern Utah church.

It is little wonder that the groups in Colorado City, Arizona, and south of the United States border in various areas, as well as in Utah and surrounding states, insist that they are the "true" Mormons and that the Salt Lake group has bowed to pressure, rather than obey their founders. Seven of the ten presidents of the Mormon Church were polygamists, as were most of the ancestors of today's Mormon leaders.

A day can come when clear-thinking youth may demand that this church either deny officially that the Lord spoke to Joseph Smith, as Section 132 of the *Doctrine and Covenants* declares, or proclaim as binding their faithfulness to their man-made ordinances and laws.

Meantime, the Utah Attorney General stated that in the Rocky Mountain area alone it was claimed in 1967 that there were thirty thousand men and women living in "sanctified" plural marriage (*Ladies Home Journal*, June 1967, p. 78). William M. Rogers, a former policeman and an investigator who studied polygamy for many years, said that there are about 100 "splinter" groups living in various forms of polygamous society (Turner, Wallace, *The Mormon Establishment*, p. 214). Many of these combine the system of communal societies with the practice of polygamy, two of Joseph Smith's plans for the form of Latter Day Saintly living.

Governmental authorities have cleared out small areas of polygamists only to find that they return. In 1953, the State of Arizona attacked the problem with a force of a hundred state troopers and served more than 122 warrants for arrest, but it creeps back. Census takers are told that plural wives are "boarders," and that the children don't give the names of their parents because they are merely shy. One leader of the cult, a man in his sixties, "married" the twelve-year-old daughter of a friend, whereas the friend, in his fifties, "married" the leader's fifteen-year old-daughter. These child brides are forced to abandon their education while they bear children, and their children will know only poverty and ignorance.

In such colonies, the people declare that they are descendants of Mormon pioneers, "followers of the great prophet, Joseph Smith," and that they cling to God's "eternal law," as set forth by "the true church." Secular authorities today consider the fundamentalists among Mormons to be part of a growing movement.

The Latter Day Saints would like us all to believe that polygamy is dead, but the closest competitor of the Utah church, the Reorganized Church of Jesus Christ of Latter Day Saints, which rejected polygamy, states:

> Repeatedly we are told that this is a dead issue—that polygamy has been renounced by the Mormon authorities and the matter need be argued no further. It is not a dead issue, nor can it be so long as their book of Doctrine and Covenants goes into all parts of the world bearing an alleged revelation which sets forth polygamy (and with equal validity concubinage) as the will of heaven and says that those who reject these document will be damned.

> This cannot be called dead so long as our friends among the Mormon missionaries everywhere defend the doctrine when pressed in argument, and often when not even questioned about it. (*Differences that Persist*, Herald Publishing House, Independence, Missouri, 1959, pp. 19-21)

A few years ago, in its European mission, the LDS church was embarrassed to learn that a number of its missionaries were openly teaching the polygamy doctrine. The LDS church excommunicated these members, although their teaching was consistent with the revelations of their prophets and holy books.

Our concern is chiefly with the theology which has caused Mormons to believe as they do. Mormons believe that spirits are awaiting physical bodies. To allow these spirits to be born is a divine mission which they must fulfill on earth. It is small wonder, then, that their adherents cling to polygamy with unshakeable faith.

The years have tempered the indignation of Americans against the paganism of polygamous habits. It is our concern, here, to awaken in some young LDS members a realization of the inconsistencies that arise when men follow *men* who embrace a man-made religion. The Bible is very clear on the subject of polygamy. In I Timothy 3:2 we read, *A bishop then must be blameless, the husband of one wife.* And Christ said, *For this cause shall a man leave father and mother, and shall cleave unto his wife: and they twain shall be one flesh. Wherefore they are no more twain, but one flesh. What therefore God hath joined together, let no man put asunder.* (Matt. 19:5-6)

The believers in "Celestial Marriage" are always at a loss to explain the words of the Lord Jesus Christ, *when they shall rise from the dead, they neither marry, nor are given in marriage; but are as the angels which are in heaven.* (Mark 12:25)

Faithful members of the Church of Jesus Christ of Latter Day Saints have a great dilemma facing them, as they study the authorized books of Mormonism. On the subject of polygamy the writings of their leader's revelations are clearly contradictory. They read in Section 132 of their *Doctrine and Covenants*:

> For behold, I reveal unto you a new and an everlasting covenant; and if ye abide not that covenant, then are ye DAMNED; for no one can reject this covenant and be permitted to enter into my glory.

The following warning is given in verse 6 of the same section:

> And as pertaining to the new and everlasting covenant, it was instituted for the fulness of my glory; and he that receiveth a fulness thereof must and shall abide the law, or he shall be DAMNED, saith the Lord God.

This section is stated to be the "Revelation given through Joseph Smith the Prophet, at Nauvoo, Illinois, recorded July 12, 1843, relating to the new and everlasting covenant, including the eternity of the marriage covenant, as also plurality of wives." The prophet had been practicing polygamy and then he "inquired of the Lord" about the matter and was given this law.

The doctrine of polygamy is actually a part of the Mormon gospel of exaltation and progression. We read in verse 32 of this same section that it is part of the many complicated Mormon rules which must be obeyed for salvation, verses 32 and 37:

> 32. Go ye, therefore, and do the works of Abraham; enter ye into my law and ye shall be saved.
> 37. Abraham received concubines, and they bore him children; and it was accounted unto him for righteousness. . . .

Can you conceive of the confusion suffered by Mormons, however, when having read the above, they then read in the *Book of Mormon*, Jacob, Chapter 2, verses 23-27:

23. But the word of God burdens me because of your grosser crimes. For behold, thus saith the Lord: This people begin to wax in iniquity; they understand not the scriptures, for they seek to excuse themselves in committing whoredoms, because of the things which were written concerning David, and Solomon his son.

24. Behold, David and Solomon truly had many wives and concubines, which thing was abominable before me, saith the Lord.

25. Wherefore, thus saith the Lord, I have led this people forth out of the land of Jerusalem, by the power of mine arm, that I might raise up unto me a righteous branch from the fruit of the loins of Joseph.

26. Wherefore, I the Lord God will not suffer that this people shall do like unto them of old.

27. Wherefore, my brethren, hear me, and hearken to the word of the Lord: For there shall not any man among you have save it be one wife; and concubines he shall have none;

And so the "holy books" as revealed to the prophet are completely contradictory, and the Mormons are literally "damned if they don't" practice polygamy and "condemned if they do." When I have pointed this out to Mormons in my meetings around the world, many of them have become greatly disturbed.

Mormon leaders used the 30th verse of Jacob 2 as a means of justifying the doctrine of plural wives:

30. For if I will, saith the Lord of Hosts, raise up seed unto me, I will command my people; otherwise they shall harken unto these things.

But this is proven false, because in the *Book of Mormon*, I Nephi 7:1, we read:

...the Lord spake unto him again, saying that it was not meet for him, Lehi, that he should take his family into the wilderness alone; but that his sons should take daughters to wife, *that they might RAISE UP SEED UNTO THE LORD* in the land of promise.

The raising up of seed unto the Lord was evidently to be accomplished by the one wife system, for according to the *Book of Mormon* Nephi stated:

And it came to pass that I, Nephi, took ONE of the daughters of Ishmael to wife;.... (I Nephi 16:7)

So, according to their own authorized "scriptures" the Lord raises up seed to Himself by monogamy, and not by polygamy. When President Wilford Woodruff (author of the Manifesto against polygamy) was questioned concerning this matter, he admitted that the Lord raised up seed by the one wife system. But, as quoted previously, God had "revealed" to their prophet Joseph Smith that if they did not abide in the law of plural wives they would be damned.

V

The Doctrine of Blood Atonement

There are pages in Mormon history so horrible that time refuses to erase their blot. They were part of the period instituted by Brigham Young as the "Reformation," totally unrelated to the Protestant Reformation of the 16th century. "Reformation," in Brigham Young's kingdom, stemmed from a period of discouragement among the people because of drought and crop ruin due to grasshoppers and their leader suffering the sting of failure from his handcart emigration plan. The tragic Handcart Scheme brought whispers of reproof from the faithful as well as condemnation from the outside world. For the "Sultan of Salt Lake" to be less than successful and to receive less than total obedience and approval from his subjects was unthinkable to this ambitious giant. Infallible he felt he must be, at any cost. And so, in order to understand the "Reformation" we must first understand the Handcart Scheme, then the "Reformation" which was the result of the inhuman doctrine of "Blood Atonement," which caused such happenings as the Mountain Meadows Massacre.

Brigham called this period not a change in their "religion," but a change in some of the practices and "lethargic habits" of the people. It was a time when power ran rampant seeking vengeful outlets. No one can understand the secrecy of the LDS church, its atmosphere of mystery, restraint, and the drawing of its people into a closed society, without knowing something of the history of this era and its strangely related chain of events.

THE HANDCART SCHEME

The train of emigrants who pushed their belongings by handcart and walked by foot across the plains and mountains in order to reach Zion has been written about in few books of history. Any who wish to learn about Mormon history and doctrine are forced to seek out the facts and sift through much misinformation. For example, a *Los*

44

Angeles Times Sunday Supplement, "West," of April 23, 1972, stated in the opening sentence of its lead article, "The Beautiful People," "A solitary cedar grew in the basin of the Great Salt Lake when Brigham Young led the first Mormon settlers in, wheeling handcarts." Those of us who have taken the time to research carefully know that the handcart method of emigration did not occur to Brigham Young until nearly ten years after the first Mormons saw the "Promised Land" in the great Salt Lake basin. Actually, Brigham began the first Mormon journey to Utah with a caravan of seventy-three wagons carrying men, three women, two children, horses, oxen, mules, cows, chickens and other needed equipment. On Brigham Young's second journey, when he led 1,229 of his people to Salt Lake, the Mormons again took in their wagons grain, three hundred pounds of "breadstuff" and all the necessary items of livelihood, as well as musical instruments to use in the evening hours of relaxation. But the European converts to Mormonism of 1856 were to be satisfied with bringing no luggage, "only a change of clothing."

This story reveals the true nature of Prophet Brigham Young as few others can. The tragic results of the handcart brigade were glossed over by such twisting of facts that intelligent readers of history can find ample proof that not only the founders of the Mormon faith, whose authority is claimed to be divine, but those leaders who followed, displayed grave evidence of error in judgment and questionable motives.

The Utah Mormons had achieved much of their success as a result of their missionary zeal. Disciples were sent to the entire globe, but were particularly successful in the European countries.

The Mormon missionary endeavors are unique, differing from those of traditional Protestant Christianity in that they built no schools, hospitals nor clinics abroad. This relieved the Utah citadel of any great financial burdens in soul-saving. To this day the missionaries are self-supporting, receiving from the LDS Church no funds or extensive missionary education for their work abroad from the Mormon Church.

Under Brigham Young, a bureau of emigration was organized and converts by the hundreds were garnered in the British Isles and Scandinavia. (Ninety thousand emigrants were attracted to America by Mormon missionaries before 1900.)

Brigham Young, as President and Prophet set up the Perpetual Emigrating Fund, to aid those without sufficient means to travel to Salt Lake. This was to tide them over until they could repay the church.

Section 16 of the fund's incorporating ordinance stated: "All persons receiving assistance from the Perpetual Emigrating Fund for the Poor, shall reimburse the same in labor or otherwise, as soon as circumstances will admit." It is noted that those who rebelled at their servitude, after they had reached Zion, were often "reminded" of their duties in this respect in Brigham's sermons.

In any case, as one Mormon writer recently mentioned: "To build their new empire—a Kingdom of God on earth—the Mormons soon realized that they would need more workers and an increased population." And the Mormon missionaries presented the emigration in such a light that it was received with great enthusiasm. This was especially true when the converts were impressed with the need to flee to Zion, as they believed the Second Coming of Christ was at hand and God's wrath would be upon the rest of the world.

In 1855, however, Young was troubled about a depression caused in Utah by a grasshopper plague which brought havoc to the crops. With the added expense on his mind of bringing the emigrants from Europe, Brigham committed a tragic blunder. He wrote to the President of the LDS European Mission:

> I have been thinking how we should operate another year. We cannot afford to purchase wagons and teams as in times past. I am consequently thrown back upon my old plan to make hand carts, and let the emigrants foot it, and draw upon them the carts, the necessary supplies, having a cow or two for every ten. They can come just as quick if not quicker, and much cheaper. . . . The carts can be made without a particle of iron, with wheels hooped, made strong and light. . . .I think we might as well begin another year at any time, and save this enormous expense of purchasing wagons and teams. . . .Of course you will perceive the necessity of dispensing with all wooden chests, extra freight, luggage, etc. They should only bring a change of clothing. Fifteen miles a day will bring them through in 70 days, and after they get accustomed to it they will travel 20, 25, and even 30 with all ease, and no danger of giving out, but will continue to get stronger and stronger; the little ones and sick, if there are any, can be carried on the carts, but there will be none sick in the little time after they get started. There will have to be some few tents. (Hafen, LeRoy R. and Ann, *Handcarts to Zion*, 1960, p. 21)

The saints in Europe were indeed given an opportunity to prove their faith. The only note of warning or realism that can be found is a poem written by Eliza R. Snow, one of Brigham Young's plural wives, and formerly a wife of Joseph Smith, the poet of the Latter Day Saints. She wrote, "A Word to the Saints Who are Gathering," saying:

> Think not, when you gather to Zion,
> Your troubles and trials are through—

That nothing but comfort and pleasure
Are waiting in Zion for you.

No, no; 'tis design'd as a furnace,
All substance, all texture to try—
To consume all the "Wood, hay, and stubble"
And the gold from the dross purify.

Franklin D. Richard, President of the LDS European Mission, described the plan glowingly, pointing out that with a handcart to every five persons, loaded with five or six hundred pounds, it would reduce the cost of emigration from Britain by two-thirds what it had previously cost. He stated, "The Hindoo devotee will suffer self-inflicted tortures of the most excruciating nature to obtain the favor of his imaginary deity. . . .Then shall not the saints who have revelations of heaven be ready to prove by their works that their faith is worth more than the life of the body—the riches of the world?" ("Millenial Star," April 14, 1855)

Brigham himself gave detailed instructions for constructing the fragile carts, which proved the major cause of the failure of the scheme. Later, Young claimed that had he given the instructions all would have ended differently, but there is adequate documentation of his very explicit orders.

Having signed the following agreement, the European saints came on eagerly. "On our arrival in Utah, we will hold ourselves, our time, and our labor subject to the appropriation of the Perpetual Emigrating Fund Company, until the full cost of our emigration is paid, with interest, if required." Accounts have stated that interest was charged. Upon reaching the United States, the emigrants were brought by railway to Iowa City, Iowa, at which point they were outfitted for the handcart journey to Utah.

Mormon missionaries acted as leaders and the groups set out, constantly delayed by the need of repairing the handcarts. As the last group approached the mountains, winter was coming on. Great numbers perished early in the journey from disease caused from crowding twenty persons into small tents. Others died from hunger and fatigue, some were devoured by wolves, and then at last, from the winter's cold, many were frozen. The courage and bravery of these staunch souls and those who led them can never be forgotten. Each morning it was necessary to count and bury the dead. Archie Walter, a carpenter from England, who almost nightly had to build coffins for those who had succumbed during the day, describes in his diary the plight of one of the first groups to "successfully" reach Salt Lake. On reaching Salt Lake he died.

To read the details of the suffering of the last handcart group enroute is an excruciating experience. The greatest disaster befell the five hundred saints led by James G. Willie, returning LDS missionary. They had had to wait near Iowa City for their handcarts. This delay, added to the fact that, when they reached Fort Laramie, Young had violated his promise and failed to send supplies, must have haunted all those responsible for the terrible loss of life. (The exact number is difficult to estimate. *The Story of America's Religions* states that 4,075 European converts pushed handcarts from Iowa to the Salt Lake Valley, but does not mention any deaths.)

Most of the local residents blamed Brigham Young, and well they might when it is remembered that he had written, "If it is once tried, you will find that it will become the favorite mode of crossing the plains; they will have nothing to do but come along." (*Millennial Star*, XVII, December 22, 1855)

The results of the handcart enterprise left Brigham Young with a severe problem. As the emigrants began their journey they had sung, "Brigham sends the word, the power to save the humble poor." Everyone had declared it Brigham's plan, and he was left with only a few choices:

1. Declare it successful in the face of the fact of disaster.

2. Blame the cause of the failure on others.

3. Claim that the emigrants were not worthy of saving or of pity.

4. Or, admit that the prophet's prophesying was sadly amiss, that "God's inspiration" was in fact man's error.

The last he could not or would not do, so he resorted to all three of the other means to regain face.

Only from his own words, in recorded speeches made during his days of dilemma, can we see the nature of the measure of the man, Brigham Young.

Remembering that every account of the handcart travelers themselves clearly showed that the cause for their delays, over and over again, was the handcart, (made too lightly out of wood, and with no iron), let us hear Brigham's first excuse; delivered at the Tabernacle, November 2, 1856, and printed in the *Deseret News*, November 12, 1856.

Br. Kimball, in his remarks, touched upon an idea that had not previously entered my mind, that is, that some of the people were dissatisfied with me and my counselors, on account of the lateness of the season's immigration. I do not know but such may be the case, as I am aware that those persons now on the plains have a great many friends and relatives here; but it never came into my mind that I was in the least degree censurable for any person's being now upon the plains.—Why? Because there is not the least shadow of reason for casting such censure upon me.

Now, hear a prophet:

This people are this day deprived of thousands of acres of wheat that would have been sowed by this time, had it not been for the misconduct of our immigration affairs this year, and we would have had an early harvest, but now we have to live on roots and weeds again before we get the wheat. . . .

If any man, or woman, complains of me or of my Counselors, in regard to the lateness of some of this season's immigration, let the curse of God be on them and blast their substance with mildew and destruction, until their names are forgotten from the earth. . . .

Last year my back and head ached, and I have been about half mad ever since, and that too righteously, because of the reckless squandering of means and leaving me to foot the bills. Last year without asking me a word of counsel, without a word being spoken to me about the matters, there was over sixty thousand dollars indebtedness incurred for me to pay. What for? To fetch a few immigrants here. . . .

Are these people in the frost and snow by my doings? No, my skirts are clear of their blood. . . .

(The above is all of the remarks made at that time, that I deem proper to print at present. B.Y.)

This note, at the end of the article in the *Deseret News*, indicated that President Young saw and edited the report of this speech before it was printed.

Two weeks later President Brigham Young delivered another address, which was printed in the *Deseret News* of November 26, 1856. This address was given a week after the arrival of the fourth Handcart group whose experiences we have related above:

. . .if people have not an opportunity of proving themselves before they die, by the rules of their faith and religion, they cannot expect to attain to so high a glory and exaltation as they could if they had been tried in all things. Yet I believe it is better for the people to lay down their bones by the way side, than it is for them to stay in the States and apostatize. . . .

If we could have it so, I would a little rather the Saints could be privileged to come here and serve the Lord, or apostatize, as they might choose, for we surely expect to gather both the good and the bad. You recollect, what I told you last Sabbath, that we can beat the world at anything. If Br. Willie the leader of the courageous fourth handcart band has brought in some of the sharks, the gatfish, the sheepheads, and so on and so forth, it is all right, for we need them to make up the assortment; as yet I do not know how we could get along without them; all these kinds seem to be necessary.

I have seriously reflected upon the gathering of the people. They have all the time urgently pleaded and importuned to be gathered, especially from the old countries where they are so severely oppressed; and they are willing to come on foot and pull hand carts, or do anything, so they can be gathered with the Saints. Well, we do gather them and where do many of them go? To the devil.

I knew all the time that it was better for many of these persons to stop in England and starve to death, for then they might have received salvation; but they plead with the Lord and with his servants for an opportunity to prove themselves, and made use of it to seal their damnation and become angels of the devil.

As to the feasibility of using handcarts, these were his sentiments:

We are not in the least discouraged about the handcart method of traveling. As to its preaching a sermon to the nations, as has been remarked, they are preached pretty nigh to destruction already. . . .Amen.

The Mormon's unquestioning obedience to authoritarian leadership caused many tragedies in their unique history. To give blind obedience to cruel and inhumane leadership is to be a part of the crimes perpetrated. This was decided by a Court of Law at Nuremburg.

Brigham Young declared, regarding the handcart tragedies, "I do not believe that the biggest fool in the community could entertain the thought that all this loss of life, time, and means, was through the mismanagement of the First Presidency." (Quoted Stanley P. Hirshon, *The Lion of the Lord*, from *Journal of Discourses*, IV, 68; Brigham Young to Erastus Snow, Dec. 7, 1856)

It was the Prophet Young blaming himself, and the rumors of the criticism among the LDS members, no doubt, that brought upon them new policies of repression. Young and his closest officials began personal interrogation of the individual members about their most personal habits. In fact, it is said that church officials called upon every Mormon family in Utah, during this time, and required that they answer these questions and state their loyalty under oath. Thus their leader was giving evidence of his own sense of insecurity.

The *New York Times* of September 9, 1877 described this time during which Young ordered a rebaptism of all the Saints. Young girls of twelve and over were required to attend lectures on the importance of polygamy, and the number of polygamous marriages performed in the temple increased greatly.

The Blood Atonement doctrine was the whip whereby the anointed leaders could give assassination orders to their people, purportedly received from God. Absolute obedience to these orders was the obligation of the members. What if they disobeyed? The Danites (Brigham Young's stormtroopers) would see to it that the blood of the disobedient was spilled "as a smoking incense to the Almighty."

Davis H. Bays wrote in his book *Doctrine and Dogmas of Mormonism*, (St. Louis, 1897, pp. 359, 360, 375):

> Nearly all the corrupt doctrines and murderous practices which later matured in Salt Lake City, including "blood atonement," or human sacrifice, killing "apostates" and murdering defenseless Gentiles—such, for instance, as the wholesale murder at Mountain Meadows—are but enlargements upon the doctrines of this revelation of July 12, 1843....The spirit of this "celestial law" — polygamy and eternal hatred of the Gentiles—permeated every branch and faction of the Mormon Church.

Whether the Blood Atonement teaching of Brigham Young sprang from Joseph Smith's polygamy revelation or from earlier or later "revelations," it was the most outrageous doctrine ever propounded by any group in this country. Before we quote from these teachings we wish to make clear that we do not contend that the Blood Atonement is part of present-day Mormon doctrine. Any good Mormon would vehemently deny that such was the case, but the question that Mormons must answer is—Why revere, immortalize, and affirm faith in such men and their revelations?

I challenge the officers of the Latter Day Saints Church to either denounce these principles and the men who fostered them, or to affirm their own belief in such doctrine.

As exhibits of the Mormon position on the doctrine of "Blood Atonement," the following extracts are taken from sermons and preachments of the Prophet Brigham Young:

> I could refer you to plenty of instances where men have been righteously slain in order to atone for their sins.
> Now, when you hear my brethren telling about cutting people

A Notorious Member of the Danite Organization

ORRIN PORTER ROCKWELL, 1813–1878

"Thus the gallows was cheated of one of the fittest candidates that ever cut a throat or plundered a traveler."—*Salt Lake Tribune.*

"Porter's life on earth, taken altogether, was one worthy of example and reflected honor upon the church."—*Apostle Joseph F. Smith.*

(Photo taken six weeks before his death)

off from the earth, that you consider it strong doctrine; but it is to save them, not to destroy them.

All mankind love themselves; and let these principles be known by an individual, and he would be glad to have his blood shed. That would be loving themselves even unto eternal exaltation.

This is loving our neighbor as ourselves; if he needs help, help him; if he wishes salvation, and it is necessary to spill his blood upon the ground in order that he be saved, spill it.

Any of you who understand the principles of eternity—if you have sinned a sin requiring the shedding of blood, except the sin unto death—would not be satisfied or rest until your blood should be spilled, that you might gain the salvation you desire. This is the way to love mankind.

It is true the blood of the Son of God was shed for sins through the fall and those committed by men, yet ye men can commit sins which it can never remit. As it was in the ancient days, so it is in our day; and though the principles are taught publicly from this stand, still the people do not understand them; yet the law is precisely the same.

Will you love your brothers and sisters likewise, when they have committed a sin that cannot be atoned for without the shedding of their blood? Will you love that man or woman well enough to shed their blood? That is what Jesus Christ meant. (*Deseret News*, April 16, 1856)

Such twisting of the gospel of Jesus Christ is blasphemy too gross for one to find words for suitable comment. They sound like the ravings of a demented man—but think how many men participated in this bloody program.

The Blood Atonement Doctrine brought anger, resentment and persecution even among the flock of the Latter Day Saints. For example, Joseph Smith's own brother, William Smith, testified in court in 1893 that as early as 1845, in Nauvoo, his life was in danger: "...if I remained there, because of my objections and protests against the doctrine of *Blood Atonement* and other new doctrines that were brought into the church." (*Temple Lot Case*, page 98)

Both male and female were to be put to death for the sin of adultery. Brigham Young stated:

Let me suppose a case. Suppose you found your brother in bed with your wife, and PUT A JAVELIN THROUGH BOTH OF THEM. YOU WOULD BE JUSTIFIED, AND THEY WOULD ATONE FOR THEIR SINS, AND BE RECEIVED INTO THE KINGDOM OF GOD. I would at once do so, in such a case; and under such circumstances, I have no wife whom I love so well that I would not put a javelin through her heart, and I would DO IT WITH CLEAN HANDS. . . .

There is not a man or woman, who violates the covenants made with their God, that will not be required to pay the debt. The blood of Christ will never wipe that out, YOUR OWN BLOOD MUST ATONE FOR IT; . . . . (*Journal of Discourses*, Vol. 3, p. 247)

The late Joseph Fielding Smith, in the book, *Doctrines of Salvation* wrote:

Joseph Smith taught that there were certain sins so grievous that man may commit, that they will place the transgressors BEYOND THE POWER OF THE ATONEMENT OF CHRIST. If these offenses are committed, then the blood of Christ will not CLEANSE them from their sins EVEN THOUGH THEY REPENT. Therefore THEIR ONLY HOPE IS TO HAVE THEIR BLOOD SHED TO ATONE, AS FAR AS POSSIBLE, in their behalf. . . (*Doctrine of Salvation*, Vol. 1, pp. 135-136)

Orson Pratt, one of the Twelve Apostles stated:

The people of Utah are the only ones in this nation who have taken effectual measures . . . to prevent adulteries and criminal connections between the sexes. The punishment, for these crimes is DEATH TO BOTH MALE AND FEMALE. And this law is written on the hearths and printed in the thoughts of the whole people. (*The Seer*, p. 223)

The above teachings of the Mormons in regard to adultery show how quick their leaders were to execute judgment and require atonement for the sin of adultery. What contrast we have here between Mormonism and the Word of God. The Gospel of John, Chapter 8, shows how the Lord Jesus Christ handled the matter of a woman, charged with adultery, being brought by the religious leaders of the day, demanding her immediate execution. How graciously the Lord dealt with the matter when He said, *He that is without sin among you, let him first cast a stone at her.* (John 8:7) Mormonism patterns itself partly after the religion of Judaism both in practice and doctrine, however, Judaism has been out of existence for more than two thousand years. A new age has been ushered in, since the time of Christ, known as the Age of Grace. Now we know, as affirmed in II Corinthians 5:19, that God is not charging the race with its sins. The sin question has been dealt with at the Cross.

It was not adultery alone, however, which brought down upon the sinners the law of Blood Atonement for their sin. Brigham Young made this statement:

If you want to know what to do *with a thief* that you may find stealing, I say KILL HIM ON THE SPOT, and never suffer him to commit another iniquity. . . . .if I caught a man stealing on my premises I should be very apt to SEND HIM HOME, and that is what I wish every man to do, to put a stop to that abominable practice in the midst of this people. . . . .I WILL PROVE BY MY WORKS WHETHER I CAN METE OUT JUSTICE to such persons, or not. I WOULD CONSIDER IT JUST AS MUCH MY DUTY TO DO THAT, AS TO BAPTIZE A MAN for the remission of his sins. (*Journal of Discourses*, Vol. 1, pp. 108-109)

Brigham Young's leaders followed the head of their church. Apostle Orson Hyde said:

It would have a tendency to place a terror on those who leave these parts, that may prove their salvation when they see the heads of thieves taken off, or shot down before the public. . . . .I believe it to be pleasing in the sight of heaven to sanctify ourselves and put these things from our midst. (*Journal of Discourses*, Vol. 1, p. 73)

The list of sins for which sinners must pay by the shedding of their own blood increased with the years. One of these sins was using the name of the Lord in vain, another was marriage to an African (according to Brigham Young, "If the white man who belongs to the chosen seed mixes his blood with the seed of Cain, the penalty under the law of God is DEATH ON THE SPOT. This will ALWAYS BE SO" –*Journal of Discourses*, Vol. 10, p. 110) "Covenant breaking" was to be condemned by the church and only atoned for by shedding of blood, as was apostasy in general.

Throughout these years Brigham Young seemed obsessed with beheading and death by knives particularly. It is recorded in the *Journal of Discourses*, Vol. 1, p. 83 that Brigham warned, "I say, rather than that apostates should flourish here, I WILL UNSHEATH MY BOWIE KNIFE, and CONQUER OR DIE." At another time Young referred to the bowie knife that he wore "round his neck." Whether these were figures of speech we do not know. We do know that there is sufficient evidence to prove that there were cases where the Blood Atonement was put into practice in the name of God. The tragedy is that the Mormon Church leaders tried to make it appear that the doctrine of Blood Atonement was taught in the Bible. The Bible teaches that the blood of Jesus Christ cleanses us from *all* unrighteousness. In I John 1:9 we read, *If we confess our sins, he is faithful and just to forgive us our sins, and to cleanse us from all unrighteousness.* The forgiveness of sins by Jesus Christ, Who atoned for the sins of all who believe, is not

Having received authority, Joseph Smith and Oliver Cowdery baptize each other in Susquehanna River, Pennsylvania.

limited to certain types of sin or their "grievousness" as the Mormon church would have us believe.

DAYS OF MADNESS

Stories of some of this madness leaked out from Utah into the country's secular press. In 1860 Horace Greeley gave some credence to the continuing rumors of threats and violence upon Utah citizens. United States soldiers were ordered to encampment near Salt Lake City and they told Greeley that "not less than seventy-five distinct instances of murder by Mormons because of apostasy . . . are known to the authorities here."

Mark Twain had repeated stories about blood atonement murders which had been told by Gentiles (non-Mormons) in which two men, Rockwell and Hickman, were named as leaders in the "Assassinations of intractable Gentiles."

It is certain that the Mormons had a "Death Society," as Elder John Hyde labeled it. This society was called by various names; in the Joseph Smith days it was known as "Daughters of Gideon," "Avenging Angels," "Destroying Angels," and at the time of the "Reformation" the group was called by Brigham Young "Sons of Dan" or "Danites," from the verse in Genesis, *"Dan shall be a serpent by the way, an adder in the path, that biteth the horse's heels, so that his rider shall fall backward. (Genesis 49:17)."*

It has been proven that the Danite idea went west with the Mormons. It is certainly believed that Brigham Young directed the Danites. We cannot here list the individual murders attributed to them. It is unfortunate that some of the men presented to Mormon young people as "heroes" were in fact murderers, because of the shocking doctrine of "Blood Atonement." Among the revered teachings of Brigham Young was the dreadful decree that sinful men could be righteously murdered in order to atone for their sins.

During the years when Brigham Young became famous, as well as infamous, many prominent men came to talk with this giant of ill repute. Many of his recorded conversations reveal his willingness to see men put to death.

Schuyler Colfax, Speaker of the United States House of Representatives, called on Brigham Young and brought with him three journalists. Young's statement that he would put two captured Confederate commissioners "where they never would peep," shocked one of these. The journalist, Mr. Bowles, wrote, "He [Brigham Young] uttered this sentiment with such a wicked working of the lower jaw and lip, and such an

**Mountain Meadows Massacre—132 emigrants killed by Mormons and
Indians.**

almost demon spirit in his whole face, that quite disposed to be
incredulous on those matters, I could not help thinking of the Mountain Meadows Massacre, of Danites and Avenging Angels, and their
reported achievements." (*New York Tribune*, July 15, 1865)

MOUNTAIN MEADOWS MASSACRE

The majority of Mormons seem uncertain of what is true concerning the Mountain Meadows Massacre. This is understandable in view of
the varied stories and perversion of facts by officialdom of the Mormon
Church. After all the years in which the church has attempted to quiet
the matter, a former Mormon is often asked, "What is the truth about
the Mountain Meadows Massacre?" No Mormon learns the truth until
he begins to search out the historical facts for himself. Unquestionably,
the doctrine of the Blood Atonement created an atmosphere of zealous
violence which led to the Mountain Meadows Massacre, often called the
outstanding American atrocity.

Other Mormon doctrines also led to such excesses. Having assumed the attributes of godliness, and consistent with the teachings of Brigham Young and Joseph Smith, it was believed that sinful men could be righteously murdered in order to atone for their sins. Such teaching is sheer madness.

The Danite code originated in the Midwest, in the days of Smith, and went West with the migrating Mormons. Brigham Young, it is equally certain, directed the Danites in their murderous missions. Inflamed with the promise that they would be gods, the faithful believers assumed the power to avenge and to take the life of their opponents or disobedient members.

In all of this there is no attempt to condemn the Mormon Church of today for yesterday's dreadful mistakes.

It was in 1857, when anger against backsliders and non-Mormons had reached a fever pitch, that a number of killings were reported by two Utah federal officials to Washington. It is said that President James Buchanan sniffed rebellion in the air. Addressing Congress, the President stated, "This is the first rebellion which has existed in our Territories, and humanity itself requires that we should put it down in such a manner that it shall be the last."

It is believed that word leaked out to the czar of Salt Lake that the Secretary of War had ordered 2,500 crack troops to march on Salt Lake. Brigham and his aides defied the government publicly. In the temple Brigham challenged the United States, "Come on with your thousands of illegally-ordered troops," he shouted in fury. "I will promise you, in the name of Israel's God that you shall melt away as the snow before a July sun."

Heber C. Kimball, ordained apostle and a close consultant to the church leadership from the days of Joseph Smith, is quoted as bragging, "Good God! I have wives enough to whip out the United States."

Just at this time Parley Parker Pratt, one of the leaders of the church, a member of the twelve Apostles and a polygamist, became involved with the wife of a non-Mormon in Arkansas. The husband, Hector McLean, charged Pratt with seducing his wife and abducting his child. Pratt, upon acquittal, was returning to Utah when the husband of the woman, Eleanor McLean, followed him and shot him. In Utah Pratt was mourned as a martyr and anger against the citizens of Arkansas is said to have been rampant.

This cannot be considered the remote cause of the Mountain Meadows Massacre, but it may, indeed, have triggered the event. The situation gradually grew more tense following the murder of Pratt and the marshaling of Federal troops.

Unfortunately, just at this time, a group of one hundred thirty-seven emigrants, led by Captain Fancher, left their homes in Arkansas and began the long trek westward to California, by way of Utah.

Most of the members of this wagon train were well behaved family people, heading west for a new and peaceful life. Along the way, however, a group of "Wildcats" from Missouri joined the party, and these "rowdies" were the spark that fired the tinder box of hate and suspicion which led to the infamy of Mountain Meadows.

The reason this sad episode is related here, in a book concerned chiefly with doctrinal vagaries of the Mormon Church, is that there is little doubt that this hideous crime, as others of its day, stemmed directly from doctrinal teachings. And in the light of vast amounts of documented evidence, I charge that the present Latter Day Saints have deliberately distorted the truth about the massacre.

No church should be condemned because of the "vile deeds" of a few of its members. But when its leaders year after year, decade after decade, attempt to cover those deeds with suppression and deceit it is only just that seekers after truth should not be denied the facts.

At various times in official publications, the leaders of the LDS Church have blamed different parties for the massacre. For example, one Mormon textbook, published by the Department of Education of the Church of Jesus Christ of Latter Day Saints (1937), *The Restored Church*, places the blame upon the emigrant train which "did much to antagonize the Indians" and upon the Indians, who it states began the attack. Belatedly the book mentions, "a number of white men also arrived upon the scene of conflict."

The account admits that "the white men" at a given signal fell upon the unarmed emigrant train, but that "hundreds of Indians" rushed upon the hapless prey." No men or women escaped the attack. All were murdered except a few children who had not been discovered. Then the official LDS statement is made, "For the deed at Mountain Meadows there is no excuse. The perpetrators were never held guiltless by the Church and the Church must not be condemned because of the vile deeds of a few of its members." (Berrett, William Edwin, *The Restored Church* Salt Lake City, 1937, pp. 484-488)

To those who do not know the truth, this may seem an honest and worthy attitude for the church to assume toward this event. In the light of available facts this is neither honest nor worthy. For example, there is the statement, "The perpetrators were never held guiltless by the Church." Ample documentation exists to prove that the known perpetrators of this hideous crime continued to hold ecclesiastical office by the vote of the church, or by appointment of its leaders, even for many years; and, as in the case of John D. Lee, even advanced from one office to a more esteemed one.

Where in Mormon textbooks is the account of the arrest and execution of John D. Lee who, twenty years after the atrocity, was made the "sacrifice" to absolve the LDS church from the scorn and righteous anger of the whole nation?

LDS President Joseph Fielding Smith wrote, in the church's *Essentials in Church History*, regarding the attack upon the emigrant train, "Lee seemed to partake of the frenzy of the redmen." If he only "seemed" to participate why was he put to death when evidence was inconclusive as to his guilt? *Essentials in Church History* also states that "other white men appeared on the scene, having been lured to the meadows with the request that their services were needed in burying the dead. Some of them remained willingly or by coercion, to participate in the massacre which followed" (Pp. 515-516). Why in all official accounts are the lawless, violent members of the Church of Jesus Christ of Latter Day Saints always referred to as "other white men"? The first Mormon publication we quoted from stated that it "is difficult to determine the entire truth." This is the most blatant of inaccuracies. A large number of writers have uncovered tremendous historical evidence upon the subject. What must the archives of the church itself contain? These are not made available to the outside world.

The niece of the late David O. McKay, president of the church, attempted to get the facts and lay the ghost of the Mountain Meadows Massacre and other uncertainties to rest. Her name is Fawn M. Brodie, and her book *No Man Knows My History*, a biography of Joseph Smith, published in 1945, was well received nationwide. But, in 1946, Mrs. Fawn McKay Brodie was excommunicated for heresy. (See *The Mormon Establishment* by Wallace Turner, Houghton Mifflin Co., Boston, 1966, p. 11). The church, promptly upon the publication of Mrs. Brodie's book, produced a pamphlet called, "No Ma'am, That's Not History," which was a vicious attack upon Mrs. Brodie's book.

Juanita Brooks, a member of the Mormon church, also wrote a book, *The Mountain Meadows Massacre,* declaring, "I am interested in the reputation of my church." For her complete study this author received a grant from the Rockefeller Foundation, "For the study of the history of the Southwest." Throughout her book, Juanita Brooks expresses her bewilderment and disbelief that her church could take the attitude it has toward this event. She states that the Mormon Church, once having taken a stand and put forth a story (that the massacre was the "crime of an individual, the crime of a fanatic of the worst stamp") feels that it should maintain that story regardless of all evidence to the contrary.

For the reader's information we quote here from the diary and confessions of John Doyle Lee, who was Indian agent for southern Utah as well as a Mormon bishop, a Danite and said to be an adopted son of Brigham Young. In that he is the "single individual" who was chosen to absolve the other Mormons of participation in the crime, his story deserves to be heard. It could be claimed that he is not a disinterested party or a witness of high integrity, but perusal of all evidence available shows his account to be amazingly factual. For this reason it is included here. Mormons, also, should remember that after the massacre Brigham Young appointed Lee judge of Washington County, and awarded him three more wives.

Portions of Lee's Confession read:

> The Mormons believe in blood atonement. It is taught by the leaders, and believed by the people, that the Priesthood are inspired and cannot give a wrong order. It is the belief of all that I ever heard talk of these things—and I have been with the Church since the dark days in Jackson County—that the authority that orders is the only responsible party and the Danite who does the killing only an instrument, and commits no wrong. . . .
>
> Punishment by death is the penalty for refusing to obey the orders of the Priesthood. About this time the Church was in the throes of a "reformation."
>
> One of the objects of the reformation was to place the Priesthood in possession of every secret act and crime that had been committed by a member of the Church. These secrets were obtained in this way: a meeting would be called; some Church leader would make a speech, defining the duties that the people owed the Priesthood, and instructing the people why it was necessary that the Priesthood should control the acts of the people; it was preached that to keep back any fact from the knowledge of the Priesthood was an unpardonable sin. . . .
>
> Brigham knew that I was not a man who liked to take life. I was well known as one that stood high in the confidence of Brigham, and was close-mouthed and reliable. I knew of many men being killed in Nauvoo by the Danites. It was then the rule that all the enemies of the Prophet Joseph should be killed, and I know of many a man who was quietly put out of the way by the orders of Joseph and his apostles while the Church was there. It has always been a well understood doctrine of the Church that it is right and praiseworthy to kill every person who speaks evil of the Prophet. This doctrine was strictly lived up to in Utah, until the Gentiles arrived in such numbers that it became unsafe to follow the prac-

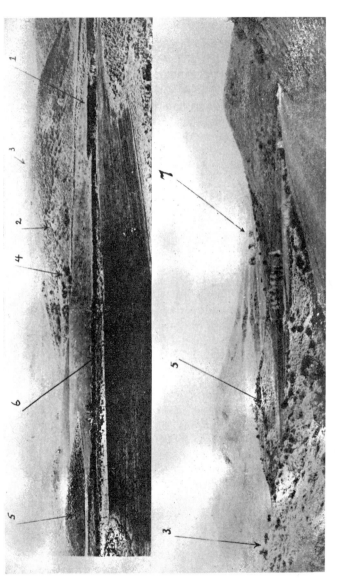

(*Above*) The Mountain Meadows (looking east): 1. Rock cairn showing location of emigrant camp and rifle pit, where some of the bodies were buried by Maj. Carlton. 2. Hiding place of some of the Indians. 3. Hamblin Ranch. 4. Bushes where two young girls were found hidden and murdered. 5. Place where the men of the party were shot. 6. The old road, now a deep gully.

(*Below*) The Mountain Meadows (looking north): 3. Site of the emigrant camp hidden by the hill. 5. Knoll (same as 5 above) where the men were shot. 7. Site of the massacre of the women and children.

tice; but the doctrine is believed, and no year passes without one or more of those who have spoken evil of Brigham being killed in a secret manner.

Lee's account of the Mountain Meadows Massacre read as follows:

> On Thursday evening, Higbee, Chief of the Iron Danites, and Klingensmith, Bishop of Cedar City, came to our camp with two or three wagons and a number of Danites all well armed. I can remember the following as a portion of those who came to take part in the work of death which was so soon to follow, viz.: [19 names followed] ... I know that our total force was fifty-four Danites and three hundred Indians. As soon as these gathered around the camp I demanded of Brother Higbee what orders he had brought. Brother Higbee reported as follows:
>
> "It is the orders that the emigrants be put out of the way. President Haight has counseled with Bishop Dame, and has orders from him to put the emigrants to death; none who is old enough to talk is to be spared.". . . .
>
> The Danites then in Council now knelt down in a prayer circle and prayed, invoking the Spirit of God to direct them how to act in the matter. After prayer Brother Higbee said:
>
> "Here are the orders," and handed me a paper from Haight. . . .
>
> Brother Higbee was then to give the order:
>
> "*Do your duty to God!*"
>
> At this the Danites were to shoot down the men; the Indians were to kill the women and larger children, and the drivers of the wagons and I was to kill the wounded and sick men that were in the wagons. . . .
>
> The Mormons were then at war with the United States, and we believed all Gentiles should be killed as a war measure, to the end that the Mormons, as God's chosen people, hold and inhabit the earth and rule and govern the globe.

The details that John D. Lee then told are too horrible to relate. The Mormons "courageously" performed their part of the blood bath, after which they took binding oaths to stand by each other, and to always swear that the massacre was committed by Indians alone. "This was the advice of Brigham," wrote Lee.

The Lee confession bears out other authorities who state that Lee had the ear of Brigham Young throughout the entire massacre. Lee served as president of the LDS colony of Harmony and presided as

elder and bishop until he resigned March 5, 1864. Immediately following the massacre he wrote that he was a delegate to the LDS Constitu-
tional Convention that met in Salt Lake City, attending throughout the
entire session, often in the company of Brigham Young, even to being
entertained in his home and treated with "kindness and consideration."
At the close of the session Lee was directed by Brigham Young to
assume charge of the cattle and other property captured from the
emigrants and "take care of it for the Indians." A year after the
massacre Lee was elected a member of the territorial legislature and the
next year, according to Lee, Brigham Young gave him and Isaac C.
Haight new wives (Lee's eighteenth). Haight was also a leader in the
massacre and a Danite.

Lee wrote:

> While in Cedar City Brigham preached one night. In his sermon,
> when speaking of the Mountain Meadows Massacre, he said, "I am
> told there are some of the brethren who are willing to swear against
> those who were engaged in that affair. I hope there is no truth in
> this report. I hope there is no such person here, under the sound of
> my voice. But if there is, I will tell him my opinion of him, and the
> fact so far as his fate is concerned. Unless he repent at once of that
> unholy intention, and keep the secret, he will die a dog's death, and
> go to hell. I must not hear of any treachery among my people."

> These words of Brigham gave great comfort. They insured our
> safety and took away our fears. . . .
> Afterwards I was arrested (on or about the 9th of November,
> 1874) and taken to Fort Cameron, in Beaver County, Utah Terri-
> tory, and placed in prison there.
> "Being the Confession of John Doyle Lee, Danite," (Lee, John
> Doyle, *The Mormon Menace*, N.Y., 1905)
> John Doyle Lee was the only member of the Mormon party
> responsible for the massacre who paid with his life for the crime. He
> was executed on Mountain Meadows, Washington County, Utah
> Territory, at the scene of the massacre, on the twenty-third of
> March, 1877. Later, standing before the monument to the slain at
> Mountain Meadows, Brigham Young quoted the Scripture, "Ven-
> geance is mine; I will repay saith the Lord," and added, "Vengeance
> is mine; I have repaid saith the Lord."*

*Sources of information on the massacre include: Military Records of the Second
Brigade, First Division, Nauvoo Legion, Copy at the Henry E. Huntington Library, San Marino, Calif.; Papers of the Attorney General prior to 1870, Records
of the Department of Justice, National Archives, Washington, D.C.; Transcript of

the Trials of John D. Lee, Huntington Library, San Marino, Calif.; Records of the Office of Indian Affairs, National Archives, Washington, D.C.; Journals and Diaries of Christopher J. Arthur, bishop at Cedar City; Miscellaneous Papers and Writings of Judge Boreman who officiated at the trials of John D. Lee; Workers of Utah, by Brimhall, Congressional Library; Records of the War Dept., National Archives, Washington, D.C.—these and many, many more are available to researchers on the subject.

VI

The Curious Declarations of
the Mormon Prophets

We are the only people that know how to save our progenitors, how to save ourselves, and how to save our posterity in the celestial kingdom of God: We are the people that God has chosen by whom to establish his kingdom and introduce correct principles into the world, and . . .we in fact are the saviors of the world. – Journal of Discourses, V. 6, p. 198

The above are the words of Mormon President John Taylor, who succeeded Brigham Young upon his death. Today, three million persons consider Brigham Young as their great prophet of God. He died at the age of 75, on August 23, 1877, their leader in religion, exploration, government, business, industry and prophecy. His funeral in the Tabernacle was attended by an estimated twelve to fifteen thousand persons. In addition to his "revelations" and large family he left an estate finally found to be in the sum of a million and a half dollars of property value. Brigham Young's son was not allowed to succeed him because of the scandals connected with his name. John Taylor, the leader of the Twelve became Young's successor.

Gradually the leaders of the church became less militant, and with the *Manifesto* removing the curse of polygamy, Mormons became more acceptable to the country's other citizens, if not vice versa. Statehood opened doors previously closed. While Utah is still strongly Mormon, politically, religiously, educationally and commercially, its vagaries have been molded into the rest of the nation.

Although the two great leaders of the Latter Day Saints had passed from the scene, their "revelations" and the "revelations" of the men who followed them are still binding upon the members of the LDS church. In fact, the revelations are, to the Mormons, laws to be obeyed. Disobedience will remove the guilty from the celestial kingdom of God.

We have discussed in part the Mormon beliefs which have caused such far reaching social and historical consequences. There are many other dogmas which are of great importance to those who would be informed about the great administrative and religious organization, the Mormon Church. Most of these are unknown to the world in general.

For example, did you know that Jesus was born in Jerusalem . . . that He was the husband of Mary and Martha . . . and that Adam was God? These are only three among many other startling doctrines to be found in the erroneous writings of Mormon leaders.

Following are some of the doctrines which differ most dramatically from Biblical Christianity. The cautious and indefinite wording of many Mormon principles lead Bible believing persons to ask, "What's wrong with these?"

"What is wrong" is that Mormon speeches and publications do not reveal, to those who do not understand the LDS vocabulary and teachings, how very unlike the Christian faith their Articles of Faith really are. It is hard to imagine how Mormon writers could so cleverly conceal the oddities of their non-Biblical teachings that the reader is deceived regarding the true meanings.

Walter R. Martin, writing for *Eternity Magazine*, substantiated this viewpoint. He said:

The statement of faith published by the Mormon Church reads in many places like a declaration of orthodox theology; however, it is in reality a clever and, I believe, a deliberate attempt to deceive the naive into believing that Mormonism is a Christian religion which it is not, in any sense of the term. . . .

Mormonism cleverly coats large doses of error with a thin layer of half-truths and seemingly plausible reasons.

Other theologians have echoed this opinion. Recently a respected scholar of another faith wrote:

Polytheism was often played down in Mormon missionary work and is generally subordinated to a more traditional emphasis in Mormon religious teaching. Yet it remains a part of the Mormon conception.

Eccentric tenets, such as Mormon belief in a multiplicity of gods, are adroitly hidden among acceptable Christian phraseology. How like the diabolical hand of Satan—the ever-present Imitator! Men will quickly reject that which is flagrantly anti-Christian or obviously con-, trary to the Bible. But men readily accept that which appears to be the faith of their fathers, expressed in Bible-paraphrased principles, particularly when accompanied by good works.

When intelligent leaders in our country, such as the Ezra Taft Bensons and the George Romneys, acclaim their allegiance and faith in Mormon doctrines, other men do not examine these doctrines closely. They will judge them by the worthy accomplishments of the adherents. Aggressive Mormonism is moving well educated young men into key positions of society on the local and national levels. Education is part of the Mormon belief in progression.

Lists of prominent Mormons are impressive: Former Secretary of Agriculture Ezra Taft Benson, and former United States Treasurer Ivy Baker Priest; former Secretary of Housing and Urban Development, George Romney. These are but a few of the many Mormon political greats. In other fields there are: Dr. Henry Eyring, chemist and author of fifty-two text books on electricity and acoustics; president of Standard Oil of California, Theodore S. Peterson; Robert Hales, senior vice-president of Max Factor; E. Cardon Walker, president of Walt Disney Productions; Ira D. Brown, president of Sav-On Drugs. Several young Mormon ladies have become Miss America or Miss American Teenager. National Young Mother of the Year for 1971 was Mrs. Billy Casper, a Mormon. Of the California Mothers Committee, recently, two of the three executive officers were Mormons and chose a Mormon as the mature-mother winner of that year. They proudly claim, "we are a competitive people." Mormons are prominent in the fields of politics, television and entertainment. The respectability of many of these fine Mormons and their devotion to their church are attracting large numbers to their impressive membership.

Everyone likes to be part of a successful organization and the LDS Church is vastly prosperous. The Mormon Church teaches that God will give material rewards to obedient and loyal members. They believe they are prosperous because they are Mormons.

The Mormon Church owns the prestigious Hotel Utah, in Salt Lake City, Deseret Book stores worldwide, the largest department store in Salt Lake, called the ZCMI (Zion's Cooperative Mercantile Institute) and many businesses in cities other than their Mecca. They own mines, railroads, vast amounts of real estate in many states and in European countries. There is no published estimate of the wealth of the church but it is said that the income from tithes alone into the church nets several millions of dollars each month.

Several years ago when the Mormon Church was considering selling a large portion of its Florida ranch lands they were priced at a hundred million dollars, and it is not known what the selling price actually was.

All of this success, which endows the Mormon Church with imperial dimensions, is influential in securing new converts to the church. Wealth, however, is not a clear indicator that God is blessing any activity or organization. The wealth of the Church of Jesus Christ, throughout history, has never been a sign of its spiritual condition.

The Apostle Paul wrote concerning the visible body of professed believers:

> But they that will be rich fall into temptation and a snare, and into many foolish and hurtful lusts, which drown men in destruction and perdition.

> For the love of money is the root of all evil: which while some coveted after, they have erred from the faith, and pierced themselves through with many sorrows (I Timothy 6:9,10).

And he warned about:

> Perverse disputings of men of corrupt minds, and destitute of the truth, supposing that gain is godliness: from such withdraw thyself.

> But godliness with contentment is great gain.

> For we brought nothing into this world, and it is certain we can carry nothing out.

> And having food and raiment let us be therewith content (I Timothy 6:5-8).

The Mormon Church is the wealthiest in the world per capita. The President, his Counsellors, the Twelve Apostles and other Mormon Church officials are wealthy men, most of whom receive large incomes from the church, although these amounts are not made public. What a contrast all of this is with the record of the true apostles of Jesus Christ, who suffered reproach and great deprivation. We read in Philippians 1:29, that Paul wrote to the saints, *For unto you it is given in the behalf of Christ, not only to believe on him, but also to suffer for his sake."*

Many ministers have sacrificed a great deal to go into the ministry and missionaries serve for a lifetime with a mere bare existence, without any thought of monetary reward, but give all for the glory of God. From the beginning of the Christian church the true ministry has been one of service and suffering:

We are troubled on every side, yet not distressed; we are perplexed, but not in despair;
Persecuted, but not forsaken; cast down, but not destroyed;
Always bearing about in the body the dying of the Lord Jesus, that the life also of Jesus might be made manifest in our body (II Cor. 4:8-10).

We mention this to contrast the life of the Apostles of Christ in the Early Church and the apostles of the Mormon Church. As we read in Paul's Epistle, I Corinthians 4:11-13:

Even unto this present hour we both hunger, and thirst, and are naked, and are buffeted, and have no certain dwelling place;
And labor, working with our own hands: being reviled, we bless; being persecuted, we suffer it:
Being defamed, we intreat: we are made as the filth of the world, and are the offscouring of all things into this day.

Although the Christian gladly serves the Lord as he is called, whether on the mission field or as a pastor, to win people to Christ or to edify the Church, there is coming a day in which the servants of the Lord will be richly rewarded:

If ye then be risen with Christ, seek those things which are above, where Christ sitteth on the right hand of God. Set your affection on things above, not on things on the earth. For ye are dead, and your life is hid with Christ in God. When Christ, who is our life, shall appear, then shall ye also appear with him in glory. (Colossians 3:1-4)

And in First Corinthians 3:12-14, we read:

Now if any man build upon this foundation gold, silver, precious stones, wood, hay, stubble; Every man's work shall be made manifest: for the day shall declare it, because it shall be revealed by fire; and the fire shall try every man's work of what sort it is.
If any man's work abide which he hath built thereupon, he shall receive a reward.

This is to take place in heaven, at the Judgment Seat of Christ, where we will not be judged as to our salvation but for the rewards by which those who have served the Lord faithfully will be recompensed accordingly.

For I reckon that the sufferings of this present time are not worthy to be compared with the glory which shall be revealed in us (Romans 8:18).

We have dealt, so far, with peculiar Mormon doctrines that have had very far reaching and sometimes tragic results. To be discussed now are some of the dogmas which grew out of the revelations of Joseph Smith regarding the church which he was to "restore."

The skeleton upon which all other Mormon beliefs take shape is undoubtedly the Latter Day Saint faith in the "Restoration."

One unacquainted with the teachings of Mormonism must ask, "What was restored, and by whom?"

First, the Mormons believe in a "restored church," quoting:

> The departure from the order, doctrine, ordinances, and spirit of primitive Christianity commenced at a very early period. . . .The Church of Christ was gone, without even a shadow of its presence to be seen upon the earth. . . .There was no inspired prophet. . . . Therefore, the ordinances of the gospel could not be administered acceptably to God, and all such ceremonies as were established among the various sects were of necessity void and without virtue in heaven. . . . Joseph Smith was the chosen instrument in the hands of God to receive the glad message and direct its promulgation to all the world. (Talmage, James E., *Articles of Faith*, pp. 33-38)

Today, Mormon missionaries (between 1960 and 1970 there were 65,215 sent; in 1971 alone, 7,256) have gone out across land and sea asking such questions as:

> Did you know that the Bible teaches that between the first and second comings of Christ there will be complete falling away from the faith once delivered to the saints; that there will be a universal apostasy, one that is so complete that the way of salvation will not be found *anywhere among any people*?

Bible students would challenge such teachings, but informed people in our own and other lands are sometimes attracted, and perhaps later won to such inaccurate and unscriptural theories.

Because of lack of information, the Mormon faith is everywhere hailed as being just a "very little different" from other Protestant denominations. We will cover at random a few of the curious declarations of the Mormon prophets which are totally different from the commandments of God as recorded in the Bible.

SEEDS OF REVIVAL

Joseph Smith informed the world that his heavenly visitors, God and His Son, told him that all existing churches were in error and "their creeds were an abomination in His sight, that those professors were all corrupt."

But how strange if Smith were asked to "restore" the Church at a time when Christianity was showing the magnificent results of revivals of the 1800's which made religious history. It is no wonder that Satan, the great competitor for the hearts of men, sowed tares among the wheat and there sprang up at this time innumerable cults.

Let us review these days in the light of our knowledge of Church history.

The very denominations named by Joseph Smith — the Methodists, Baptists and Presbyterians figured most actively in the great revivals of the 1800s.

A year after young Joseph Smith's alleged heavenly visitation, Charles G. Finney was converted and, in 1824, ordained by the presbytery. His revivals began in 1825, and concerning these, Finney's one-time critic, Dr. Lyman Beecher said, "This is the greatest work of God and the greatest revival of religion that the world has ever seen in so short a time." And Robert O. Ferm writes, in his *Cooperative Evangelism* (1958), "The test of time gives credence to the abiding effects of the Finney revival and bears witness to the fact that this man was anointed of God an evangelist."

There were others, such as Moody and Sankey. So powerfully was the Holy Spirit at work vitalizing the Church in these days that it has been said of D. L. Moody that he took two continents in his hands and rocked them.

Those who believe in total apostasy must ignore the historical fact that the revivals of the 1880s were so long in continuance and so lasting in influence that to estimate their results numerically would be impossible. In Kentucky alone, it was known that ten thousand persons were added to the Baptist churches of that one state during the revivals, and there was scarcely a religious denomination which did not share in the great fruits of this evangelism.

It is not surprising that the hosts of Satan viewed their losses with alarm and desired to "confuse the elect" with substitutes which were based upon counterfeits of the men of God and the Word of God.

In New England the revivals had produced such consequences that whole cities were moved and changed. In Boston and New York, revivals were preceded by the famous noon prayer meetings, where, in the heart of the cities, men and women poured out of their homes and places of business daily in the spirit of repentance—and the result was regeneration for vast numbers of souls.

Then revival moved west. By 1820 the United States possessed all the territory west of the Mississippi to the Rocky Mountains, with the exception of the California region and Texas, which were claimed by both the United States and Spain. Awakened and regenerated American Protestantism saw this as one great mission field. Formation of the United Domestic Missionary Society was the first step in a new home mission work. "Spurred on by the revival preaching of Beecher, Finney, and a host of others, the east continued to pour out funds to save the west. There was not a territory overlooked. All the denominations were conscious of their responsibilities." One contemporary author has said of these days that the Great Revival of the early nineteenth century produced "sinners converted to action, ready to lead the onslaught against the forces of evil."

In May, 1830, representatives of eight of the largest denominations met in New York City, feeling that in association was strength and these groups drew on the strength of hundreds of thousands of members. Beecher said these groups "constitute a sort of disciplined moral militia, . . . by this auxiliary band . . . the land is purified, the anger of the Lord is turned away." The new life of the Spirit pulsated through the churches and released by revivalism brought forth home and foreign mission boards.

In 1812, the American Board of Commissioners for Foreign Missions was formed to find ways and means for promoting the spread of the Gospel in heathen lands. In 1812, five famous missionaries sailed for India. They brought the first rich fruits by inspiring other dedicated men and women to follow them in winning the world for Christ. In a short time the Presbyterians cooperated with the American Board, as well as the Dutch Reformed Church, and the work expanded. The Baptists established a General Missionary Convention in 1814. Methodists and Episcopalians founded missionary societies and sent many men overseas. Dr. A. M. Chirgwin, in his book *The Bible in World Evangelism,* tells us that this evangelical revival sent ripples to the end of the earth. "It transformed the face of Christendom and showed Christianity for the first time in generations as a dynamic religion, claiming the whole world for its Lord. It swept forward in breath-taking strides. Indeed, the hundred years following the Evangelical Revival have been called by Professor Latourette the 'great century' in view of the fact that it witnessed the greatest expansion of Christianity since the days of the Apostle." And then this author describes the formation in Europe and Britain of their great missionary societies, the North American missionary enterprises, formed between 1810 and 1820, and makes note of the American Bible Society founded in 1816.

Of course the young Joseph Smith spoke out of ignorance with his condemnation of Christianity of his day, and it is acknowledged that he gathered his group of leaders out of malcontents, religiously speaking. Nevertheless, succeeding officials of the Mormon Church have not all been ignorant of the history of Christianity. For them to continue to toss aside the lives of men like Spurgeon, Judson, Rice, Livingstone, and hosts of others with the continuous repetition of the claim that "all their creeds were an abomination in God's sight," and that "those professors were all corrupt" is an insult to Protestantism and its Spirit filled warriors of the Cross. Mormon missionaries should meet Protestants who are aware of their great Christian heritage, and willing to defend it against the claim of "total apostasy."

In essence Mormonism treats with almost equal contempt the great heroes of the Reformation and the days that followed it. For we must remember how they insist that Joseph Smith "was a prophet of God; that he was inspired as no other man in his generation, or for centuries before . . . that he had been chosen of God to lay the foundations of God's Kingdom as well as of God's Church." (*Gospel Doctrine*, Salt Lake City, 1928, p. 624)

But the Church, which the Mormons declare was non-existent, pressed on with new fervor. Missions were not the only new outpouring of religious enterprise. The tremendous energy tapped by revivals were released in many Christian movements in the early nineteenth century which were on a national scale—the Sunday school movement, temperance groups, Bible societies. Christian education was not neglected. In 1800 there were only two genuine colleges west of the Alleghenies, but by 1830 that number grew to twenty-six. In the knowledge that an educated lay people would require an educated ministry, seminaries were built; the Church built schools of theology and divinity. All of this evidenced the vitality and energy of nineteenth century Protestantism in America. Men like Finney were converting thousands from deism. It is said of Finney that his sermons were like lawyer's pleas, and he did not encourage extreme emotionalism. All the great eastern cities fell under his sway and in New York City the Broadway Tabernacle was built for him. Many such men were presenting redemption through Jesus Christ and souls were saved by a great outpouring of the Holy Spirit.

In spite of the marvelous spirit of evangelism of that day, Joseph Smith dared to say that his "visitors" maintained that "the Church of Christ was gone, without even a shadow of its presence to be seen upon the earth."

THE CHURCH RESTORED

Joseph Smith was, according to his own story, told that he was to join none of the churches of his day. Then, after three years, Joseph declared that the heavens opened again and an angel, Moroni, appeared and instructed him that night and the following day. "According to the word of the Lord to Joseph Smith the continent of America was given to Joseph and his posterity as an everlasting inheritance" (Smith, Joseph Fielding, *The Restoration of All Things*).

The prophet convinced his followers that God had told him that he should "restore" the church, and that God had chosen Joseph as the instrument for the restoration.

A RESTORED PRIESTHOOD

There was to be a "restored church," a "restored priesthood," and a "restored gospel." The Mormon priesthood has been called by some, "an illustration of religious autocracy scarcely duplicated in the history of mankind." It was "restored" in an era when democracy was blossoming in this free nation "under God," a priesthood to command the people in secular matters as well as spiritual. Its leaders make short work of the nation's founding father's belief in separation of church

Statue on the Temple grounds at Salt Lake City, depicting John the Baptist bestowing the Aaronic Priesthood upon Joseph Smith and Oliver Cowdery.

and state. Said the late President of the Mormon Church, Joseph Fielding Smith, regarding a man's personal freedom, "When a man says you may direct me spiritually but not temporally, he lies in the presence of God."

It is inconceivable that anyone who claims knowledge of the Bible would *wish* to restore the Levitical priesthood: *Seeing that we have a great high priest, that is passed into the heavens, Jesus the Son of God* (Hebrews 4:14).

The writer of the Epistle to the Hebrews was speaking to a group which was deeply dyed with the doctrines and practices of Judaism and he clearly set forth the superiority of Christ over the order of the Levitical priesthood. It is not difficult to understand how those early Jewish converts, steeped in the traditions of their fathers and prejudiced against any simpler order of worship might find it difficult to forsake those things which their fathers had held holy for generations. Many of these Jews were, no doubt, sincere believers in Christ, but they wanted to retain their familiar forms and ceremonies, their temple and its priesthood functions. Thus the book of Hebrews, so clearly written by the inspiration of the Holy Spirit, came down to men today who again are reaching back to things which God has removed. That Bible-reading men can again fall into this trap, wishing to become spiritual Israelites, rather than accept the superiority of Christ to all man-made systems of redemption is inexplicable. The author's reply to the Mormon restoration of the priesthood will be found in his answer to the Fifth Article of Mormon Faith, in the chapter which follows.

All of the complicated systems which men can devise to work out their own salvation, are swept away by one clear, full look at the glory, the completeness, the sufficiency of Christ; He had "finished" all these things for us.

Howbeit in vain do they worship me, teaching for doctrines the commandments of men (Mark 7:7).

Nevertheless, the Mormon Church claims that it is the only one having the authority and priesthood to administer the ordinances of the Gospel. The church further claims that on May 15, 1829, John the Baptist conferred the *Aaronic Priesthood* on Joseph Smith and Oliver Cowdery. Section 13 of the *Doctrine and Covenants* is cited as evidence that the Aaronic Priesthood was given to Smith and Cowdery, but this section did not appear in the revelations as they were originally printed in the *Book of Commandments* (which is not now available through the

Utah church, but only through the bookstores of the Reorganized Church of Latter Day Saints, Independence, Mo.).

The *Melchizedek Priesthood*, it is claimed, was organized by Peter, James and John, although the exact date of this appearance to Smith is not stated. This too is absent from the *Book of Commandments* published in 1833, but was added to the *Doctrine and Covenants* at a later date.

We know that after Joseph Smith alleged that the disciples conferred the Melchizedek Priesthood upon him, he stated concerning a conference held in June 1831. "...the authority of the Melchizedek Priesthood was manifested and conferred for the first time upon several of the elders" (*History of the Church*, by Joseph Smith, Vol. 1, pg. 175-176).

Whatever the origin of this authoritative group, it was referred to by Stanley P. Hirshon, in his book *The Lion of the Lord* (p. 20) who said, "The Mormons, moreover, developed a group of Melchizedek priests as militant as the Jesuits." Mr. Hirshon also states the premise that had not Joseph Smith developed the priesthood hierarchy, which expanded his organization almost without his further efforts, his church and his doctrines might have perished.

BAPTIZING FOR THE DEAD

Under the authority of the Melchizedek Priesthood one of the most unusual practices of the Mormon Church takes place in the temples— the baptism for the dead.

In the Book of Malachi, the 4th chapter, we read:

> *Behold, I will send you Elijah the prophet before the coming of the great and dreadful day of the Lord: And he shall turn the heart of the fathers to the children, and the heart of the children to their fathers, lest I come and smite the earth with a curse —(verses 5 and 6).*

The Mormon Church claims that Elijah the Prophet appeared in the Kirtland Temple, in the early days of Mormonism, and opened the "door of salvation" for those who are dead, thus fulfilling this prophecy.

> The work done by Elijah was to open the door of salvation for the dead (*History of the Church*, Introduction to Vol. 2).

Upon careful examination we find that verses 5 and 6 of the 4th chapter of Malachi could not apply to an appearance of Elijah in the

Kirtland Temple because the Bible makes it very clear that this prophecy is to be fulfilled in the coming "Day of the Lord."

To answer those who ask, "What do Mormons teach today concerning baptism for the dead?" we refer to the LDS Church publication, *The Improvement Era*, October, 1960 issue, in which the late President Joseph Fielding Smith answers an inquiry concerning their "Sacred Secret Covenants," saying:

> In the Book of Mormon we find the clearest statement on the resurrection of the dead ever revealed to man. Let it be remembered that there are some truths made manifest in our sacred covenants that are not intended for the world. These naturally do not appear in the Book of Mormon. The Savior taught his disciples many things which they were not to reveal to the world which belong solely to those who have made their covenants in righteousness. Things of this kind do not appear in the Book of Mormon, or in the Bible, or any other published book.
>
> If there is no reference in the Book of Mormon in relation to baptism for the dead, we ask the question why should there be? Is not baptism for the dead exactly the same principle that it is for the living? The answer is naturally "Yes."

We find here a Mormon leader attempting to explain the natural questions of his people regarding a custom which is not even included in their own "holy book" and which can be Bible-related only by misconstruing such Scriptures as I Corinthians 15:29 and I Peter 3:18-21. Reading further from the above article:

> There is no baptism for the dead until after the resurrection of our Lord. This ordinance for the dead was not performed until Jesus had opened the way. Therefore if there is no mention of baptism for the dead in the Book of Mormon, that does not prove that they, after the resurrection of Jesus, could not, in cases where it was necessary, perform such ordinances, since they had the fulness of the priesthood.

We learn at this point that the "secret covenant" of baptism for the dead is understood by Mormons when the phrase of "The Fulness of the Gospel" is used. It is little wonder that non-Mormons are often confused by Mormon writings and preachments, because there are many meanings understood by Mormon adherents alone, which are clothed in phraseology, acceptable though confusing, to the outsider. Quoting Mr. Smith further:

Then we should remember that for some two hundred years after the visitation of the Lord to the Nephite nations, all observed the principles of the gospel.

It is our responsibility to perform all the ordinances essential for the dead, no matter when they lived or when they died, from the time of Adam down to the present time. We have been taught that this is *our* responsibility and that the Lord in his due time, after we have done all in our power, will make it possible by revelation for the salvation of all the worthy dead through all ages of time. The great work of the millennium will be this labor.

This criticism here raised by a member of the class, has come up for discussion periodically in past years. Can we not put an end to this fruitless and unnecessary discussion?. . .

Although not included in the original *"Book of Commandments,"* it was later claimed that with the coming of John the Baptist and Peter, James and John to the Prophet Joseph and Oliver Cowdery, they were given the keys to the Priesthood, and the authority to act "in God's name" in administering the rite of baptism "by water and by Spirit."

An official publication, "Why Mormons Build Temples," published by the Mormon Church, describes the temple work from its inception:

The Latter Day Saints were taught by their prophet that celestial glory could be theirs in the eternal world, but only through "obeying the celestial law, and the whole law too."

Speaking to his people on April 8, 1844, the Prophet Joseph said that the temple ordinances as he was giving them were so important that "without them we cannot obtain celestial thrones. But there must be a holy place prepared for that purpose."

Temples built in latter days are equally sacred and, therefore, they too are reserved only for the most faithful members of the Church.

The great Mormon temples are, however, opened to the public for viewing when they are first built, before temple ordinances have been performed there. After the buildings are dedicated and the usual activities of temple work are begun, no visitor is ever admitted again.

Of interest to visitors at the temples is the baptismal font. In each temple this font rests upon the back of twelve immense stone or bronze oxen. It is said that this is according to the instructions given to Joseph Smith by the Lord.

In his book *The Restoration of All Things*, the late President Joseph Fielding Smith enlarges on this subject:

> There is historical evidence that the ordinance of baptism was administered in behalf of the dead. Paul confirms the doctrine of salvation for the dead in this same epistle to the Corinthian saints in these words: "If in this life only we have hope in Christ, we are of all men most miserable." Moreover, the Savior declared that some sins would be forgiven after death to those who do not blaspheme against the Holy Ghost.

The claim is that the Lord said to Joseph Smith:

> All who have died without a knowledge of this gospel, who would have received it if they had been permitted to tarry, shall be heirs of the celestial kingdom; also all that shall die henceforth without a knowledge of it, who would have received it with all their hearts, shall be heirs to that kingdom, for I, the Lord, will judge all men according to their works, according to the desires of their hearts.—*Hist. of the Ch.* 2:380.

Then, the Mormons proceed with the program of baptism for the dead, under the assumption that the "worthy dead" would have accepted the gospel with all its ordinances, and therefore the ordinances will have to be performed in behalf of the dead, although vicariously. They believe that the Lord declared to Joseph Smith that such vicarious blessings were "ordained and prepared before the foundation of the world, for the salvation of the dead who should die without knowledge of the gospel." (Smith, Joseph Fielding, *The Restoration of All Things*, see pp. 229-235).

So the vast operation began with God revealing this doctrine to the Prophet Joseph Smith, who was told that the baptism for the dead should be performed in God's holy house. It is stressed that God had this ordinance in mind when He commanded the Latter Day Saints to build temples.

The alleged statement of the Lord is, "For a baptismal font there is not upon the earth, that they, my saints, may be baptized for those who are dead" (*Doctrine and Covenants* 124:29-39).

A week following the dedication of the Kirtland Temple, Elijah appeared to Joseph Smith and Oliver Cowdery in the temple and gave them the keys of sealing power, that all ordinances for the dead could be validly performed, claim the Mormons.

> Thousands and tens of thousands of genealogical records have been compiled. The spirit of turning the hearts of the children to

their fathers has swept the whole earth since Elijah came to accomplish his promised mission. While this spirit cannot be seen, the operation thereof has touched the hearts of men and women the world over. They do not know why they are compiling genealogical records, yet this work has made rapid strides—really it is "a marvellous work and a wonder" in and of itself. . . .

Already the Church of Jesus Christ of Latter Day Saints has one of the best genealogical libraries in the world. They have recently been microfilming many of the genealogical records of the nations of Europe (Christiansen, El Ray, "The Primary Purpose of the Present Dispensation," *The Improvement Era*, June, 1960).

And so the search for ancestors knows no bounds. Tons of genealogical records are purchased by the church's Genealogical Society each year. A German collection was purchased composed of 7,000,000 names from hundreds of thousands of individual family groups. Elder Myers, superintendent of the Society, estimated that it would require five hundred years to administer the ordinances for the names in this collection in the Swiss Temple, if the present rate of endowment work there was doubled. The freight bill alone on the shipment exceeded $2,500. Permission was given to microfilm a collection of records from *The Times* library in London. Another gift to the Society from England comprised two tons of books. The article in the Mormon publication, *The Instructor*, of March, 1961, describing these "finds," began, "Millions and millions of names. . .and all he was looking for was a few ancestors."

The ceaseless search is intensified as the years go by, successive generations remembering or being reminded that President Wilford Woodruff gave warning:

Since God is no respecter of persons, he will not give privileges to one generation and withhold them from another. The whole human family, from Father Adam down to our day, have got to have the same privileges somewhere, of hearing the Gospel of Christ. They have to be preached to in the spirit world. But nobody will baptize them there. Therefore, someone must administer to them by proxy here in the flesh, that they may be judged according to man in the flesh and have part in the first resurrection.

In their publications LDS leaders warn, "We have to enter these temples and redeem our dead. This is the great work of the last dispensation, the redemption of the living and of the dead. . . ."

The *Improvement Era* magazine, previously referred to, put stress on the importance of family ties:

We as heads of families must not equivocate in this; we must not procrastinate; we must not assume that Aunt Martha or some other relative is doing all that needs to be done in this respect. Members of the Church are coming to the temples in ever-increasing numbers. For some time the average number of endowments administered on behalf of the dead by the good people in this temple district, has averaged 1738 endowments a day, besides the sealings and the baptisms. Nearly 40,000 were administered during the month of March in the twenty-three days during which the temple was open. The same thing is going on in all the temples. . . .When I see busy men nearly equaling the number of women, coming hurriedly from their offices, and from their work, regularly by appointment to act in behalf of these who have passed beyond, it touches my heart. . . .

The other phase of our responsibility, however, that of identifying the dead through genealogical research, is barely keeping pace with the work done in the temples of the Lord. In this temple we have for some time administered many more endowments for the dead than we have baptisms for the dead. That means that we will eventually run into difficulties if something is not done in the matter of more extensive research on the part of the individual families.

. . .For I tell you, none of us can expect to bathe in glory if we have "gone it alone" and have not reached out a hand for others in this respect.

What this program means to the church in a financial way is impossible to estimate. We do know to what lengths it can be carried. It is reported that children are required to be baptized for at least fifteen dead persons in order to go "up" in their organization, and some have been immersed as many as one hundred fifty times in one day.

Literally millions are being spent by the Mormons for this total effort. Someone is said to have been baptized for every pope of the Catholic Church, and for all the presidents of the United States, with the possible exception of three. (These were neglected because of their treatment of the Mormons.) One Mormon admitted he had been baptized over five thousand times for the dead. It is claimed by Mormons that their temples are built to last throughout the millennium and that during the thousand-year period, they will proceed to baptize, by proxy, all of the dead of the past ages who have not had a chance to respond to the "restored gospel."

MORMON ARCHIVES

Southwest of Salt Lake City, about 20 miles, can be seen four immense tunnels (or more) which house the Mormon archives. These are an impregnable bomb shelter and storage vault for the genealogical records of the church. Costing millions of dollars, these tunnels are blasted out of the solid granite as deep as 600 feet into the mountainside. Church officials claim that the vaults are built to last forever, and that even atomic disaster could not disturb the church records. Humidity within the vaults is controlled at a constant temperature which will keep the records "safe through the millennium."

The Mormons explain that the living can be baptized elsewhere, but only the font in the temple is for the vicarious baptisms in behalf of the dead. They say, "If baptism is so essential for the salvation of the living, is it less essential for the salvation of the dead?"

Is this a Christian doctrine?

The Mormons use I Corinthians 15:29 in attempting to prove that it is. This and other Scriptures relating to this subject are thoroughly discussed in the portion of Chapter VIII of this book entitled, "Can We Save the Dead?"

It has been interestingly remarked by one non-Mormon writer that Mormon ideas concerning baptism for the dead seem to appeal most to those who have a feeling of guilt about their deceased. This I have known to be true, in specific instances, where an individual suffers because he has failed to witness to a loved one or be zealous in good example and prayer. When the loved one is taken in death, the unconsolable spouse has been known to turn to the Mormon Church solely upon this doctrine. What a fragile reed upon which to rest—man's reasoning, man's doctrines, man's performances.

Feverishly they are seeking among genealogical records for the names of those known and unknown, for whom they may perform an act of redemption. What trickery Satan employs, when all about us souls are perishing for want of hearing the Gospel of Christ. Our Lord said, "Why seek ye the living among the dead?"

The immensity of this program is described by a Mormon Bishop, who writes:

Some time ago the architect who designed the vaults pointed out that the Mormons' collection of genealogical records—the most extensive collection in the world—contained more than five hundred million pages of names and dates. While the church claims expenses connected with the Genealogical Society that run into the millions each year, there are no amounts mentioned for the sums received from the faithful for this work for the dead.

The late Dr. Ironside quotes one of the elders of the Mormon Church as saying to him that "Through baptism for the dead the Mormons have saved more souls than Christ did when He died on the cross."

Mormon teachers would have one believe that both Christ and Paul taught baptism for the dead, using I Corinthians 15:29 as their authority. It seems most clear that Paul was referring to an existing ritual and merely asking rhetorically why they were baptizing for the dead, if they did not believe in the resurrection. Roman Catholic theologians, whose rituals we would feel were more nearly like Mormonism than any other, also take issue with the Mormon position on this subject. One scholar has written a very complete exegesis, which we can only report in part:

> Joseph Smith, the patriarch of the Mormons, commanded his followers to keep a diligent record of any Baptism they administered or which was received in the Mormon temple. The book of these records will be the book of life from which people are to be judged according to Apocalypse 20:12 (J. Smith, *Doctrine and Covenants*, Sect. 128, nos. 1-5, Salt Lake City, Utah: 1848, p. 232). "Now," he says to his followers, "the nature of this ordinance consists in the power of the priesthood, by the revelation of Jesus Christ, wherein it is granted that whatsoever you bind on earth shall be bound in heaven, and whatsoever you loose on earth shall be loosed in heaven. Or, in other words, taking a different view of the translation, whatsoever you record on earth shall be recorded in heaven, for out of the books shall your dead be judged, according to their own works whether they themselves have attended in their own *propria persona,* or by means of their own agents. . . . (*Doctrine and Covenants* 128:8).
>
> Joseph Smith's interpretation of "to bind" as meaning "to write a record" is entirely arbitrary. And to say that the earthly and material book of those records corresponds to the allegorical, heavenly book of life, is the fruit of "revelations" or of dreams, not of exegesis. . . .
>
> If the Mormons suppose that the unbaptized dead now want to accept the Gospel and be baptized through the works of their proxies, they contradict Scripture which teaches that "it is appointed unto men once to die, and after this the judgment" (Hebrews 9:27). . . .
>
> For these reasons we find Mormon Baptism for the dead entirely erroneous and arbitrary. (Foschini, Fr. Bernard M. "Those Who Are Baptized for the Dead," An Exegetical Historical Dissertation, Mass., 1951).

It has, we feel, been noteworthy to include one Roman Catholic's opinion on this subject—a subject in which Romanism and Mormonism do have a somewhat similar interest. In the maze of Mormonism there are many turnings which were first taken by Roman Catholicism. It is obvious to the Bible student who acquaints himself with the Mormon system that there are many similarities between these two massive religious movements. Within the limits of this book we cannot devote a lengthy portion to the many parallel teachings of Rome and Salt Lake. We pause to point out only a few. Both are temple builders, developing monolithic organizations which rule by their authoritative priesthood. They both proudly claim that theirs is the only "true" church, whose leader is the very mouthpiece of God. Their followers are induced into obedience to church-made rules and observances which take pre-eminence over civil regulations. Their ceremonial practices are shrouded with mystery and elaborate symbolism.

With all the vast sums spent and the time consuming effort involved in genealogical searching and in baptizing for the dead it is seldom pointed out to the Mormon people that both the Bible and the *Book of Mormon* state that such efforts are futile. In the Book of Alma (*Book of Mormon*) we read:

> Ye cannot say, when ye are brought to that awful crisis, that I will repent, that I return to my God. Nay, ye cannot say this; for that same spirit which doth possess your bodies at the time that ye go out of this life, that same spirit will have power to possess your body in that eternal world (Alma 34:34).

The Bible makes clear that no one can redeem another:

> *None of them can by any means redeem his brother, nor give to God a ransom for him (Psalm 49:7).*

The Bible warns, in the Book of Titus 3:9:

> *Avoid foolish questions, and genealogies, and contentions, and strivings about the law; for they are unprofitable and vain.*

CELESTIAL (TEMPLE) MARRIAGE

In reviewing the peculiar practices of the Mormon Church, we have mentioned the ordinances "restored" to this earth. One which is little understood is the belief in "Celestial Marriage." It is called the "crowning Gospel ordinance," and, like baptism for the dead, appears to be one of the reasons the Mormon Temples are so important and secretive.

Joseph Smith explained that marriage "till death do ye part" is a man-made system, and that with the restored gospel the saintly glory was to be one, "Which shall be a fullness and a continuation of the

The entrance to the Mormon Temple, Salt Lake City, where
LDS members go to perform the rituals of baptizing for the
dead and celestial marriage.

seeds forever and ever." He explained that "the Gods" were to be
parents of spirit children "just as our Heavenly Father and Heavenly
Mother were parents of the people of this earth."

A portion of section 132 of the Mormon *Doctrine and Covenants*
reads:

Mormons going to the Temple for baptismal ceremony
for the dead.

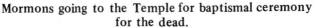

Except a man and his wife enter into an everlasting covenant and be married for eternity, which in this probation, by the power and authority of the Holy Priesthood, they will cease to increase when they die; that is, they will not have any children after the resurrection. But those who are married by the power and authority of the Priesthood in this life, will continue to increase and have children in the celestial glory.

Thus we see that celestial marriage is the crowning Gospel ordinance. If men and women have obeyed this holy ordinance and all the other principles of the Gospel, following the resurrection and the great judgment day, *then shall they be Gods.*

A number of authors have expressed the doubt that Joseph Smith would have declared this doctrine to his people had he not had polygamy in mind. The Reorganized Church of Jesus Christ of Latter Day Saints, of Independence, Missouri, which refused to accept Brigham Young as prophet and broke away from the large body of Mormons, does not accept Celestial Marriage, but says:

This idea of human progression through and under the law of celestial marriage and polygamy is correlated with the idea of a progressive God and has roots in the document on "celestial marriage" and polygamy accepted by the Mormons as a divine revelation. It has no roots at all in our law of theology. . . .In their edition of the book of *Doctrine and Covenants*, this alleged revelation stipulated that if a man marry a woman according to this law and this "new covenant" and do not commit murder, "to shed innocent blood," they shall come forth in the next world to inherit thrones and kingdoms, and dominions (Smith, Elbert A., *Differences that Persist,* Independence, 1959, p. 12).

Mr. Elbert Smith then quotes from the Utah *Doctrine and Covenants* 132:19 in which Mormons are to receive glory which "shall be a fullness and a continuation of the seeds forever and ever."

The late Joseph Fielding Smith was quoted in the *Deseret News Press* (Salt Lake) from his radio talks in 1944, reiterating the celestial marriage position of Joseph Smith, almost word for word, adding "all covenants, contracts, bonds, obligations, oaths, vows, performances, connections, associations, or expectations, the Lord has said, which are made by man shall come to an end, for only that which the Lord has sanctioned shall endure forever." It is the teaching of the Church of Jesus Christ of Latter Day Saints, as we have said, that we all lived in the world of spirits before we came to earth and became clothed in bodies of flesh and bones. Therefore, said the late Joseph Fielding

Smith, "God not only commends but he commands marriage. Those who have taken upon themselves the responsibility of wedded life should see to it that they do not abuse the course of nature, that they do not destroy the principle of life within them, nor violate any of the commandments of God. The command which he gave in the beginning to multiply and replenish the earth is still in force upon the children of men. MALE AND FEMALE ENTER HEAVEN. No man will ever enter there until he has consummated his mission; . . . . The woman will not go there alone, and the man will not go there alone, and claim exaltation. . . . .They cannot be exalted in any other way, neither the living nor the dead. It is well for us to learn something about why we build temples and why we administer in them for the dead as well as the living." (Smith, Joseph Fielding, *Gospel Doctrine*, Selections from the Sermons and Writings, Salt Lake City, 1928).

It has been a source of amazement to me that Mormon women so vigorously defend and cling to these doctrines when we know that in reality the Mormon husband is believed to be the "savior of the Mormon woman." He alone has the authority to call her forth in the resurrection. All one has to do is to attend the funeral of a Mormon wife to know that, when most of the congregation has left, the Priest places the veil over the dead woman's face, to be there until her husband calls her forth in the resurrection.

Strangely, or perhaps logically according to Mormon doctrine, the connection between baptism for the dead and celestial marriage is part of the theology of the LDS church.

It is also clear that both of these practices are flourishing in Mormon temples today. From time to time, LDS members become aware of the full teachings of the church and study God's Word. One of these was Mrs. Freda Sterling, who lived in New Zealand. The practices of baptism for the dead and celestial marriage were her major reasons for leaving the Mormon church. She wrote:

> This is the stark reality of things! The aim, ambition and glory of Mormon priesthood being an imagined mass procreation. And this not in a hazy spiritual sense, but physical, as a hallmark of absurdity, held that in the celestial realm they will have human bodies, complete with all physical potentialities and desires. . . .
> What is right in their celestial kingdom is equally right on earth, as the lesser is invariably contained in the greater. If this is denied they are placed on the horns of a dilemma, as this thing cannot be had both ways: and Mormon leadership knows this full well. No alteration or evasion of formerly accepted statements or mental reservation can eradicate this conclusion.

It can be taken for granted that the only hindrance to the advocacy and practice of plural marriage is civilized and Christian law; otherwise the examples set by Brigham Young and his like would, where possible, be followed.

When I realized that one of the two pagan reasons for the erection of their temples is for the perpetuation of the repulsive idea of celestial marriage, and that our names were to be sealed to that end, I fought for freedom. We had been led into their lair; we had held offices; encouraged people into the movement; had been held up as examples for others to follow; and now we were on the verge of repudiating the delusion that had obsessed our lives. The President of the New Zealand Mormon area pleaded with us not to do so. But I felt there was something wrong, devilishly wrong, and I wanted right. I wanted light and truth; I wanted liberty from the Mormon chain; I wanted Christ. And find them I would! It took three months of negotiation, and only after legal threat did the President agree to meet me on the issue. His attitude can be well understood, as losing us, others would follow in our steps; others who like us had gone into Mormonism without investigating what it really stood for; its misleading Articles of Belief, its fraudulent foundation and imitation prophets and priests, its antagonism to God's Word and pagan superstitions. Yes, he had much to fear. And as it is, many are questioning whether this thing is a delusion from the Devil. May they be led from its darkness to the light, from this satanic power to God. . . .

Mrs. Sterling became a Christian shortly after she left Mormonism. She discovered that Christ was able to satisfy her heart's need. He was sufficient. In her own words she states:

. . . I experienced such an extraordinary change within me that the past of Mormonism faded. Gone were its false prophet and President; Gone were its priests and elders; gone its absurd doctrines and control. Instead I had the Lord, His Word and His peace. What more did one need!

Neither is there salvation in any other [Prophet or Priest] : for there is none other name under heaven given among men, whereby we must be saved (Acts 4:12).

The unique practices of the Utah Mormon Church which have been stressed in this chapter will be discussed in the light of the Bible Scriptures in a chapter to follow, entitled "Wresting the Scriptures, The Bible or the Book of Mormon."

THE NEGRO QUESTION

A very serious problem faces the Mormon Church today because its leaders have consistently denied to the Negro the priesthood (so prized by all the members). The peculiar theological stand on the discrimination practiced by the LDS Church against the Negroes is a deep study in itself. There are few outside the Mormon faith who understand why it is so ingrained in the principles of Mormonism. There is a reason that a belief that some are born more noble than others is compatible with Mormon doctrine. One of the basic doctrines of the Mormon Church is that the spirit of man existed before the world was created. Joseph Smith once stated, "the Soul, the mind of man, the immortal spirit, all men say God created it in the beginning. The very idea lessens man in my estimation; I do not believe the doctrine. . . .The mind of man is as immortal as God himself. . . .God did not have power to create the spirit of man at all" (*Times and Seasons,* Vol. 5 p. 615).

The Apostle Orson Pratt declared, ". . .the spirits of men and women, all had a previous existence, thousands of years ago. . .and I have already told you that among them are many spirits that are MORE NOBLE, more intelligent than others. . ." (*Journal of Discourses*, Vol. 1, p. 62).

When, at last, the Mormon Church was forced to change its position and grant blacks the rights and privileges of "receiving the Priesthood," there was considerable stir in the press nationwide. Had it not been referred to as "One of the few uncracked fortresses of discrimination" by the press? *(Los Angeles Times,* Aug. 27, 1967).

Among the Latter Day Saints there was an even greater stir.

Had not an Apostle in the Mormon Church written, "Negroes in this life are denied the priesthood; under no circumstances can they hold this delegation of authority from the Almighty. The gospel message of salvation is not carried affirmatively to them . . . Negroes are not equal with other races where the receipt of certain spiritual blessings are concerned . . . . " *(Mormon Doctrine,* 1958, page 477).

Had not the First Presidency stated clearly in a letter written July 17, 1947: "From the days of the Prophet Joseph even until now, it has been the doctrine of the Church, never questioned by any of the Church leaders, that the Negroes are not entitled to the full blessings of the Gospel." (Letter from the First Presidency, quoted in *Mormonism and the Negro,* by John J. Stewart and William E. Berrett, pp. 46-47).

Joseph Smith himself, their founder and "Revelator," had revealed to them in the *Book of Moses,* that "the Lord set a mark upon Cain . . . and there was a blackness came upon all the children of Canaan."

Brigham Young had affirmed that the blacks could not hold the Priesthood saying clearly that the blacks could not hold the Priesthood until *after* the resurrection: "Cain slew his brother . . . and the Lord put a mark upon him, which is the flat nose and black skin. . . . How long is that race to endure the dreadful curse that is upon them? That curse will remain upon them, and they never can hold the Priesthood or share in it until all the other descendants of Adam have received the promises and enjoyed the blessings of the Priesthood and the keys thereof. Until the last ones of the residue of Adam's children are brought up to that favorable position, the children of Cain cannot receive the first ordinances of the Priesthood." He left no room for any modern day Priesthood to change this revelation, stating:

> When all other children of Adam have had the privilege of receiving the Priesthood, and of coming into the kingdom of God, and of being redeemed from the four quarters of the earth, and have received their resurrection from the dead, then it will be time enough to remove the curse from Cain and his posterity . . . he is the last to share the joys of the kingdom of God. (*Journal of Discourses,* Vol. 7, pp. 290-291 and Vol. 2, p. 143).

As recently as 1967 the First Presidency of the Mormon Church reaffirmed the teachings of Brigham Young and N. Eldon Tanner was quoted as saying:

> The church has no intention of changing its doctrine on the Negro. Throughout the history of the original Christian church, the Negro never held the priesthood. There's really nothing we can do to change this. It's a law of God. *(Seattle Magazine,* December, 1978, p. 60).

Another Mormon apologist, John L. Lund, wrote, in 1967:

> Social pressure and even government sanctions cannot be expected to bring forth a new revelation . . . all the social pressure in the world will not change what the Lord has decreed to be. . . .
> The prophets have declared that there are at least two major stipulations that have to be met before the Negroes will be allowed to possess the Priesthood. The first requirement relates to time. The Negroes will not be allowed to hold the Priesthood during mortality, in fact, not until after the resurrection of all of Adam's children. The other stipulation requires that Abel's seed receive the first opportunity of having the Priesthood. . . . Negroes must first pass through mortality before they may possess the Priesthood ("they will go down to death"). Reference is also made to the condition that the Negroes will have to wait until after the resurrection of all of Adam's children before receiving the Priesthood . . . the last of Adam's children will' not be resurrected until the end of the millennium. Therefore, the Negroes will

not receive the Priesthood until after that time ... this will not happen until after the thousand years of Christ's reign on earth ....

The second major stipulation that needs to be met ... is the requirement that Abel's seed receive the opportunity of holding the Priesthood first. *(The Church and the Negro,* 1967, pp. 45-48).

The leadership of the LDS Church was faced with a dilemma of great proportions. All of their prophets must be accepted by their members as infallible, their revelations coming directly from God. Somehow the Mormons had survived the reversal of the church's position on polygamy — although some still continue to practice polygamy in communes in sparsely populated areas. They defend their position boldly on the basis that it was a revelation to their prophets from God. How were the leaders now to explain that their divinely inspired prophets were in error?

Why must they do this? Obviously the government would be requiring complete equalization of racial privileges in order for them to maintain their tax exempt status. Also young Mormons were confronted with the "Negro Question" in their missionary endeavors around the world. Their church's teachings became increasingly unpopular as the Mormon Church had become a growing, extremely visible worldwide organization. How, for example, were such teachings consistent with their immensely popular tourist attraction in Hawaii, their Polynesian Cultural Center? There, young Mormon converts of all races produced a winsome example of their LDS movement.

Christianity teaches, "God is no respecter of persons" (Acts 10:34). How could the LDS church retract their belief in inequality of the races?

Very simply, the First Presidency of the Church of Jesus Christ of Latter Day Saints released the following statement, on June 9, 1978:

As we have witnessed the expansion of the work of the Lord over the earth, we have been grateful that people of many nations have responded to the message of the restored gospel, and have joined the Church in ever-increasing numbers. This, in turn, has inspired us with a desire to extend to every worthy member of the Church all of the privileges and blessings which the gospel affords.

Aware of the promises made by the prophets and presidents of the Church who have preceded us, that at some time in God's eternal plan, all of our brethren who are worthy may receive the priesthood; and witnessing the faithfulness of those from whom the priesthood has been withheld, we have pleaded long and earnestly in behalf of these, our faithful brethren, spending many hours in the upper room of the temple supplicating the Lord for divine guidance.

He has heard our prayers, and by revelation has confirmed that the long-promised day has come when every faithful, worthy man in the Church may receive the holy priesthood, with power to exercise its divine authority, and enjoy with his loved ones every blessing that flows therefrom, including blessings of the temple. Accordingly, all worthy male members of the Church may be ordained to the priesthood without regard for race or color. Priesthood leaders are instructed to follow the policy of carefully interviewing all candidates for ordination to either the Aaronic or Melchizedek Priesthood to insure that they meet the established standards for worthiness.

We declare with soberness that the Lord has now made known His will for the blessing of all His children throughout the earth who will hearken to the voice of His authorized servants, and prepare themselves to receive every blessing of the gospel.

Of course the LDS Church hoped this would mean only a small crack in the credibility of its prophets, living and past. The fact that this church is a secretive organization where opposition receives very little publicity aided the Mormons in this momentous decision. But there was consternation.

A class at Brigham Young University conducted a "random telephone survey" of Utah County residents and found that 79 percent of the people had not expected such a change, at least at this time. By some, the news was reported to be as shocking as the announcement of an international disaster. Forty-five percent of those interviewed expressed the doubt that the news was true. Forty percent said that they did not expect this to happen until years in the future, during the Millenium or after Christ's return. Some said that they felt as if there had been a death in the family. It appeared that Mormons realized the serious implications in such a doctrinal change.

Their most vocal leaders were busy making statements. Apostle Bruce R. McConkie explained that the old teachings concerning blacks were given "without the light and knowledge that now has come into the world." "Forget everything that I have said, or what President Brigham Young or President George Q. Cannon or whomsoever has said in days past that is contrary to the present revelation. . . . We have now added a new flood of intelligence and light on this particular subject, and it erases all the darkness and all the views and all the thoughts of the past. They don't matter any more. It doesn't make a particle of difference what anybody ever said about the Negro matter before the first day of June of the year (1978)." (*Are All Alike Unto God,* Apostle Bruce R. McConkie of the Council of Twelve, pp.1-2). Confusing? What other words of their leaders should be "forgotten"?

Eager young students would apply logic to such statements. If this is the case, what about other unscriptural revelations? A seemingly small crack may presage a mammoth deluge upon the walls of doctrinal adherence. Pride in scholarship has marked young Mormon's eagerness for service. Youth involvement has been the bulwark of LDS success. We can only pray, that if this momentous decision regarding the blacks causes doubt to permeate the minds of Mormon youths, that they will turn to God's Word as the one, true revelation, guide and authority. May all their members understand that "other foundation can no man lay than that is laid, which is Jesus Christ" (I Corinthians 3:11).

How vastly different are these teachings on the subject of race from the teachings of the Word of God. We read in Acts 10:34 that "God is no respecter of persons." We call the readers' attention to the well known verse in the Gospel of John, Chapter 3, verse 16:

> For God so loved the world that he gave his only begotten Son, that *whosoever believeth in him should not perish, but have everlasting life.*

The word "whosoever" means, "anyone, without exception," excludes no one. It crosses all lines and man-made divisions. It does not put up barriers between the good and the bad, the rich or poor, white or black. It is *"whosoever."*

JOSEPH SMITH AND THE "PEARL OF GREAT PRICE"

The Book of Abraham, allegedly translated by Joseph Smith, was published in 1842 and is now a part of the *Pearl of Great Price*, one of the four standard works of the Mormon Church.

Today, the Mormon leaders find themselves faced with a serious problem. An article appeared in the *New York Times*, July 15, 1968, authored by Wallace Turner, a non-Mormon, a Nieman Fellowship recipient who studied at Harvard and in 1966 was the author of the book *The Mormon Establishment*. The *New York Times* article read:

> SAN FRANCISCO, July 14—Papyrus fragments about 2300 years old have created bitter wrangling among intellectuals of the Mormon world. The argument is theological and archeological, but it could turn sociological by undermining the scriptural basis for the Mormon's discrimination against Negroes.
>
> Since the Metropolitan Museum of Art in New York gave the fragments to the Church of Jesus Christ of Latter-day Saints last November, the ancient documents have reopened old disputes about the divinity of the inspiration of Joseph Smith Jr., the Mormon prophet.
>
> The papyri are part of an Egyptian scroll acquired by the Mormons in 1835 and translated by Smith as the Book of Abraham, one of the Mormons' sacred works. . . .

Mr. Turner is correct in saying that this controversy uncovers a sociological problem for the Mormons, i.e. the refusal of full membership rights to the Negro; for Mormon Prophet David O. McKay stated, in 1947, "I know of no scriptural basis for denying the Priesthood to Negroes other than one verse in the Book of Abraham (1:26); however, I believe, as you suggest, that the real reason dates back to our preexistent life." (Quoted in *Mormonism and the Negro*, by John J. Stewart and William E. Berret, Part 2, p. 19).

Joseph Smith the prophet made this statement concerning these rolls of papyrus, ". . .I commenced the translation of some of the characters or hieroglyphics, and much to our joy found that one of the rolls contained the writings of Abraham. . . ." (*History of the Church*, Vol. 2, p. 236.) Joseph Smith's story was that he had acquired some papyri, which, when he had translated it, was found to be the Book of Abraham. He claimed that Abraham had written this book on papyrus thousands of years ago. In 1842 he published it and the Mormons accepted it as scripture. Needless to say, when the papyrus were discovered and given to the Mormon Church, the Mormon people were elated, feeling that Joseph Smith's story had been vindicated.

Many of the knowledgeable leaders of the church, however, advised their people to be cautious. Dr. Sidney B. Sperry, of the Brigham Young University, stated, ". . .as members of the Church we ought not to overrate the importance of this discovery." (Newsletter and Proceedings of the Society for Historic Archaeology, Brigham Young University, Provo, March 1, 1968, p. 8.)

Dr. James R. Clark said, in the same publication, "I agree with the point of view, Dr. Sperry." He warned that there was great danger for the church in "claiming too much" too soon.

Dr. Hugh Nibley, a top Mormon authority on the Egyptian language, had earlier warned:

> "The papyri scripts given to the Church do not prove the Book of Abraham is true." Dr. Hugh Nibley said in an Academics Office-sponsored assembly, "LDS scholars are caught flat footed by this discovery." (*Daily Universe*, Brigham Young University, Dec. 1, 1967.)

It appears that Dr. Nibley and a few others may have realized that the papyri could not be used to prove Joseph Smith's work true, for when it was presented for examination to learned Egyptologists the opinions were that these were fragments of the *Book of Breathings*, a traditional copy of the Shaiten Sensen, probably written in the Ptolemaic Period (after 332 B.C.). Two of the most prominent experts in this field in the United States have confirmed this indentification. John A. Wilson, Professor of Egyptology at the University of Chicago, made this statement: "Document D is a related mortuary text of late times, the so-called *Book of Breathings*," and Richard A. Parker, Chairman of the Department of Egyptology at Brown University, confirmed the fact that what Joseph Smith claimed was the Book of Abraham was in reality the *Book of Breathings*.

Dr. Nibley, speaking at the University of Utah, May 20, 1968, raised many questions relating to Smith's translating the papyri, "By what process could the Book of Abraham have been squeezed out of a few brief signs? Nobody has told us yet. Was Joseph Smith really translating the papyri? If so, it was not in any way known to Egyptology. Was he then merely pretending to translate them? But he never put these symbols forth as his source. . . ." (From an article written for the Brigham Young University Studies) The dialogue on the subject goes on and on. Students say that Dr. Nibley "wants us to ignore the evidence which the 'Sensen' fragments furnish and wait for years while he searches, through 'bushels of nonsense' and 'legends' hoping that he may find something that may be used as evidence for the Book of Abraham."

What does it all matter? If Joseph Smith was not translating, by his miraculous means, the Book of Abraham, but, in fact, an ancient Egyptian *Book of Breathing*, concerning the dead, the church is obligated to repudiate the Book of Abraham. If the Book of Abraham is repudiated, the anti-Negro discriminatory practices have no basis for existence.

The Reorganized Church of Jesus Christ of Latter Day Saints (of Independence, Mo.) has never accepted the two books of the *Pearl of Great Price* as divinely inspired. Wallace Turner, referred to previously, the author of *The Mormon Establishment*, quotes a member of the Reorganized Church as saying, "I guess you could say that we look on Joseph Smith as a prophet, and that we also look on him as a man."

THE MORMON PROPHET DESCRIBES OUTER SPACE

One of the most bizarre revelations of the Prophet Joseph Smith, which must have filled the people of his day with astonishment, is in regard to the inhabitants of the moon. The prophet was indeed specific, stating:

> The inhabitants of the moon are more of a uniform size than the inhabitants of the earth, being about six feet in height. They

dress very much like the Quaker style and are quite general in style, or the fashion of dress. They live to be very old: coming generally near a thousand years. (*Journal of Oliver B. Huntington*, a devout Mormon contemporary of Joseph Smith. Copy at Utah State Historical Society, Vol. 2, p. 166 and also one in the Henry E. Huntington Library, Pasadena, California.)

This "revelation" concerning the moon and its inhabitants was not the only information which Joseph Smith gave in regard to outer space. During his years in Nauvoo, he made known another "revelation from God" concerning portions of the earth being "torn asunder" and "borne away to form another sphere and planet to hide Enoch and also the "lost ten tribes." He told of great portions of the earth being taken up out of the "northern waters" and from "where the Gulf of Mexico now exists," which "naturally threw the earth out of balance."

Eliza Roxey Snow, Joseph Smith's sixteenth wife, wrote a hymn concerning these phenomena and when asked where she acquired this astounding information she answered, "Why, my husband the Prophet Joseph, told me about it. This Hymn 322 of the "Sacred Hymns and Spiritual Songs for the Church of Jesus Christ of Latter-day Saints" 1891 ed.

Hymn 322

Thou, earth, wast once a glorious sphere
Of noble magnitude,
And dist with majesty appear
Among the worlds of God.

But thy dimensions have been torn
Asunder, piece by piece,
And each dismembered fragment borne
Abroad to distant space.

When Enoch could no longer stay
Amid corruption here,
Part of thyself was borne away
To form another sphere.

That portion where this city stood
He gained by right approved;
And nearer to the throne of God
His planet upward moved.

And when the Lord saw fit to hide
The "ten lost tribes" away,

Thou, earth, wast severed to provide
The orb on which they stay.

And thus, from time to time, thy size
Has been diminished, till
Thou seemst the law of sacrifice
Created to fulfill.
    —Eliza Roxey Snow

The acceptance of Joseph Smith as a true prophet of God is a requirement of the Mormon faith. In the Mormon doctrinal book, the *Doctrine and Covenants*, it is stated, "Wherefore, meaning the church, thou shalt give heed unto all his words and commandments which he shall give unto you as he receiveth them, walking in all holiness before me; For his word ye shall receive, as if from mine own mouth, in all patience and faith" (Sec. 21:4,5).

In that Smith's words are to be received "as if from the mouth of God" and his prophecies and revelations accepted as authoritative, then by what standard or criterion should Smith and his words be tried in order to determine if he speaks the words of God? The only universally acceptable standard is the Bible.

In Deuteronomy 18:21,22 we read, *And if thou say in thine heart, How shall we know the word which the Lord hath not spoken? When a prophet speaketh in the name of the Lord, if the thing follow not, nor come to pass, that is the thing which the Lord hath not spoken, but the prophet hath spoken it presumptuously: thou shalt not be afraid of him.* If Joseph Smith were a true prophet of God, then all his prophecies and revelations would be consistent with the Bible and would come to pass just as predicted.

Joseph Smith's prophecies concerning outer space were made at a time when he felt assured that no earth man would ever visit the moon. Now that our men have been to the moon, it is obvious to anyone that visions such as the Mormon prophet recorded are blatantly foolish and false.

The facts we have been bringing to the readers' attention may seem to be minor matters, and they are not mentioned for the purpose of bringing attack on the character of Joseph Smith. Many sordid details of history have been omitted. The importance of these "revelations" of the prophets is that members of the LDS church are forced to endorse them *in toto* as a requisite of membership. Brigham Young went so far as to say, "Every intelligent person under the heavens that does not, when informed, acknowledge that Joseph Smith, jun., is a Prophet of God, is in darkness, and is opposed to us and to Jesus and his kingdom on the earth" (*Journal of Discourses*, v. 8, p. 223).

Some readers of the Joseph Smith story pause at the very opening, when his first vision is described. (Joseph claimed that this appearance to him of the Father and the Son occurred when he was 14, but 18 years passed before these visions were recorded.) Most Christians have read in the Bible (John 1:18) that *No man hath seen God at any time.* They are also familiar with I Timothy 6:16 where, describing the Son, Jesus Christ, the King of kings, and Lord of lords, the Apostle states, *Who only hath immortality, dwelling in the light which no man can approach unto; whom no man hath seen, nor can see: to whom be honour and power everlasting.*

Did God and the Son appear to Joseph Smith? Every Mormon will answer this question with a decisive, "Yes." But when we give a careful look at the Bible in relation to such possibility one is forced to choose where truth really lies.

The verses we have quoted above are describing the fact that the mortal eye cannot look on the true essence of God. Just as a person cannot look with unshielded eyes at the sun, in all of its brilliance, so man cannot see the fulness of God the Father or God the Son (in His ascended glory) unless the "unapproachable light" is diffused, "toned down" to man's "sight level." When Moses asked God, "Show me thy glory" (Exodus 33:18) he little realized what he was asking. God gave Moses the privilege of viewing His "back" (Exodus 33:23), His receding glory. So it is that without dark glasses men can only look upon the sun when it is setting on the horizon. So it was also that Moses, Isaiah, Jacob, Abraham and others saw God in a "specially adapted" form of God's own choosing. These appearances of God are known as "theophanies," and have little in common with the reported appearance of God the Father and God the Son to Joseph Smith.

> *But there were false prophets also among the people, even as there shall be false teachers among you, who privily shall bring in damnable heresies, even denying the Lord that bought them and bring upon themselves swift destruction (II Peter 2:1).*

VII

Mormon Articles of Faith

After reading the Articles of Faith of the Mormon Church, many Christians conclude, "This reads like sound doctrinal belief." The problem of Mormonism lies in the fallacies, in the light of the Bible, which are concealed within the Articles of Faith or in the two other authorized books of Mormon Faith, the *Doctrine and Covenants* and the *Pearl of Great Price*. Doctrinal difficulties are further compounded in that these books often differ on vital principles of faith. The very first Article of Faith is an excellent example of the dilemma which confronts searchers after truth.

ARTICLE I

We believe in God, the Eternal Father, and in His Son, Jesus Christ, and in the Holy Ghost.

This would appear to be a simple statement of faith in the Triune God. The truth is that Mormons do not believe in the Trinity, but do, in fact, believe in a multiplicity of gods.

Joseph Smith taught the doctrine of the "plurality of gods" and openly ridiculed those who stood firm to the Bible revelation that there is only One God.

> I will preach on the plurality of Gods. . . .I have always declared God to be a distinct personage and a Spirit: and these three constitute three distinct personages and three Gods. . . .Many men say there is one God; the Father, the Son and the Holy Ghost are only one God! I say that is a strange God anyhow—three in one, and one in three. . . .All are to be crammed into one God, according to sectarianism. It would make the biggest God in all the world. He would be a wonderfully big God—He would be a giant or a monster. (Smith, Jos. F. *Teachings of the Prophet Joseph Smith*, pp. 370-372.)

While the *Book of Mormon* is explicit concerning the Godhead (*Alma 11:28, 29)* "Now Zeezrom said: Is there more than one God? And he answered, "No." and the fact that God is a Spirit, *And then Ammon said: Believest thou that there is a Great Spirit? And he said, Yea. And Ammon said: This is God."* *Alma 18:26-28*), at a later date Joseph Smith taught differently. By 1844 he had completely disregarded the teachings of the *Book of Mormon* on the subject. He claims, by making the Book of Abraham authoritative, that now there are "Gods." See Abraham 4:3, 10, 25: 5:8, in which the *And I God* of the Book of Moses is changed to *And The Gods.* . . ." The Mormon *Journal of Discourses* is filled with statements by Mormon Apostles (such as Orson Pratt, Heber C. Kimball, and, of course the Prophet Brigham Young) that there are many gods.

The *Teachings of the Prophet Joseph Smith*, by the late Joseph Fielding Smith, reveals that Joseph taught, "In the beginning, the head of the Gods called a council of the Gods; and they came together and concocted a plan to create the world and people it" (p. 349).

Then, although the claim of Joseph Smith is that he saw two Personages, the Father and the "Beloved Son," the prophet later contradicted this story and said that he saw the mother of God and Jesus (whom he calls the "Lamb of God" and the "Eternal Father"). The first claim is in the *Pearl of Great Price* stating that Joseph "saw two Personages, whose brightness and glory defy all description, standing above me in the air. One of them spoke unto me calling me by name, and said, pointing to the other—*This is my Beloved Son. Hear Him* (p. 48, v. 17)! Then in the *Book of Mormon*, the contradiction reads: "Behold the virgin which thou seest, is the mother of God." ". . .behold the Lamb of God, yea, even the Eternal Father!" ". . .and Jesus Christ, which is the Lamb of God. . . ." If Jesus Christ is God the Eternal Father, according to this, how could Joseph Smith have seen "two personages"?

The early founders and prophets seemed uncertain whether there were two or three members of the Godhead because their teachings about the Holy Ghost are neglected in the greater part of their authorized doctrinal books. It is true that William E. Berrett quotes Joseph F. Smith as saying, "The Holy Ghost is a Personage of Spirit, he constitutes the Third Person in the Godhead." (*The Restored Church*, p. 541, 1956 ed.) And on page 540 of this book Mr. Berrett states, "The Holy Ghost is a person. Unlike the Father and The Son who have bodies of flesh and bone, the Holy Ghost has no body of flesh and bone (that is, of the elements as we know them) but is a personage of spirit."

It is obvious that in addition to believing in many gods, the

Mormons maintain that God the Father and God the Son have mortal bodies, in other words they are taught that God is an anthropomorphic god. The Mormon Church leaders taught also that it was necessary to have a body of flesh and bone in order to attain eternal progression. Joseph Fielding Smith did not let the matter of the Holy Ghost having to do without a body be a problem to him, stating, "I have never troubled myself about the Holy Ghost whether he will sometime have a body or not because it is not in any way essential to my salvation. (*Doctrines of Salvation,* Vol. 1, page 39.)

A Roman Catholic scholar studied the Mormon's concept of God, gods and man, all developing and changing in a developing universe, as compared with the Christian concept of a transcendent, unchanging God. He remarked that the Mormon repudiation of the creationist theology was a repudiation of spirituality in favor of materiality. He quoted, "Mormonism has elaborated an American theology of self-deification through effort, an active transcendentalism of achievement," and then commented, "All this is expressed in their belief of advancement of intelligences toward perfection. Man 'cooperates' with God in the tightly knit authoritarian priesthood organization." (O'Dea, Thomas F., *The Mormons,* Chicago, 1957.)

The patriarchal system developed by the Mormons includes loyalty and obedience to family, the priesthood, and to their humanized God. To this is added the aspirations toward godhood in man. As Joseph F. Smith wrote, "The Lord designed our coming and the object of our being. . .like him we may be filled with pure intelligence, and like him we may be exalted to the right hand of the Father, to sit upon thrones and have dominion and power in the sphere in which we shall be called to act." (Smith, Joseph F., *Gospel Doctrine,* Salt Lake City, 1928).

As preached by Delbert L. Stapley of the Council of Twelve and quoted in *The Improvement Era* (Mormon magazine):

> As sons and daughters of God, we are required to purify and perfect ourselves in righteousness; otherwise, we cannot be with him nor enjoy eternal lives and glory in his kingdom. To become like God we must possess the powers of Godhood.

These teachings have come faithfully down from the founding fathers of the Mormon church:

> ETERNAL LIFE — April 7, 1844. "Here, then, is eternal life—to know the only wise and true God; and you have got to learn how to be Gods yourselves, and to be kings and priests to God, the same as all Gods have done before you, —namely, by going from one small degree to another, and from a small capacity to a great

one; from grace to grace, from exaltation to exaltation, until you attain to the resurrection of the dead, and are able to dwell in everlasting burnings, and to sit in glory, as do those who sit enthroned in everlasting power."

That which is without body, parts and passions is nothing. There is no other God in heaven but that God who has flesh and bones.

IS THE MORMONS' GOD THE HISTORIC GOD OF THE BIBLE?

(1) Their god is one of many gods. While the Mormons do not believe in the Trinity, they have, since the days of Joseph Smith, believed in a plurality of gods. *But the first of the Ten Commandments is, "Thou shalt have no other gods before me"* (Exodus 20:3).

(2) *Their god is a changing god.* Brigham Young taught, "The God that I serve is progressing eternally, and so are his children. . ." (*Journal of Discourses*, Vol. 1, p. 93). Or, as the Apostle Orson Hyde said, "Remember that God, our heavenly Father was perhaps once a child, and mortal like we ourselves, and rose step by step in the scale of progress. . ." (*Journal of Discourses*, Vol. 1, p. 123). Joseph Smith led the way in such teachings:

> I am going to tell you how God came to be God. We have imagined and supposed that God was God from all eternity. I will refute that idea, and take away the veil, so that you may see. It is the first principle of the Gospel to know for certainty the character of God and to know that we may converse with him as one man converses with another, and that he was once a man like us; yea, that God himself, the father of us all, dwelt on earth, the same as Jesus Christ did. . . . (Smith, Joseph, *—King Follett Discourse*, a funeral oration recorded, Salt Lake City).

But in Malachi 3:6 we read, *For I am the Lord, I change not. .;"* As the Psalmist said, "Before the mountains were brought forth or ever thou hadst formed the earth and the world, *even from everlasting to everlasting, thou art God."*

(3) *Their god is mortal, a god of "flesh and bone."*

> The church offers the knowledge to man that the Almighty has been a man also. . . .He is resurrected, glorified, exalted being with a body of flesh and bones. (Sperry, Dr. Sidney B., Professor of Religion, Brigham Young University, *The Improvement Era,* Aug. 1947, Vol. 50, p. 510).

> The Father God is a man of immortal tabernacle. . .of flesh and bone as tangible as man's (*Doctrine and Deity*, p. 26, Roberts).

Today's Mormons are equally emphatic upon the subject of a god who is man-like and that men are to become godlike. From the Deseret Book Company, Salt Lake City, come the writings of Timberline W. Riggs, entitled *A Skeptic Discovers Mormonism*, in which Mr. Riggs stated in 1941 (Fourth Edition 1946):

> There is no confusion about God's Word. Neither is there any confusion about Him. Learn to know Him as Man Perfected. As such He has revealed Himself to us through His Scriptures. He is the Perfect Man you and I may become through obedience to law. . . (p. 26).

A contemporary of Mr. Riggs, Bruce R. McConkie of the Mormon Council of Seventy, stated his faith in a man-like, anthropomorphic god, "The other churches believe in a God without body, parts and passions, who fills the immensity of space. . .God is a person. He is in one place at a time. He is man." (McConkie, Bruce R., *Standard Examiner,* Ogden, quoting from a speech, June 5, 1950).

When I was a young boy, attending Sunday School in the Mormon Church, I was taught, "Christians worship a strange God. He is so vast he fills the universe and so small he dwells in the human heart." At this point the class would laugh, believing the Mormon god, of flesh and bone, to be far superior to the God of historic Christianity.

The Lord Jesus Christ stated, *God is a Spirit: and they that worship him must worship him in spirit and in truth* (John 4:24).

In the unique Mormon concepts of God we must also mention that Brigham Young taught the Godhood of Adam.

IS ADAM GOD?

Concerning Adam, Brigham Young stated, "He is our Father and our God, and the only God with whom we have to do." (*Journal of Discourses* Vol. 1, p. 50.) This doctrine brought much confusion and strife.

Brigham Young is quoted in the Mormon *Millennial Star*, during this time of dissension among the faithful, concerning the Adam-God theory, as saying:

> Concerning the item of Doctrine alluded to. . .that Adam is our Father and God, I have to say do not trouble yourselves, neither let the Saints be troubled about the matter. . .If, as Elder Caffall remarked, there are those who are waiting at the door of the Church for this objection to be removed, tell such, the Prophet and

Apostle Brigham Young has declared it, and that it is the Word of the Lord (*Millennial Star*, Vol. 16, p. 543).

Brigham Young continued to teach this doctrine, for we read a statement quoted in the *Deseret News* from one of Young's sermons just a few years before he died (1873), "How much unbelief exists in the minds of the Latter-day Saints in regard to one particular doctrine which I revealed to them and which God revealed to me—namely that Adam is our Father and God. . ." (*Deseret News*, June 14, 1873).

Modern Mormon writers attempt to explain this doctrine without denying it. Milton R. Hunter, in his book *The Gospel Through the Ages* (Salt Lake City, 1945, pp. 68, 69) writes:

> Since he was foreordained to be the father of the human family, Adam was appointed by the Saviour to hold the keys of the Priesthood throughout all Gospel dispensations until the Son of Man should come to reign. Therefore, whenever the Priesthood has been withdrawn from the earth through apostasy, the keys have been brought back from heaven by Adam's authority. . . .
>
> Just prior to the second coming of the Saviour, an important council meeting will be held at Adam-Ondi-Ahman, Missouri. Jesus, Michael, Gabriel, and all the great high priests who have held the keys of the Priesthood from Adam's day down to this dispensation will be in attendance. At this meeting, Adam will surrender his authority—or the keys of the Priesthood—to Christ, but will retain his standing as head of the human family. He will be crowned as the prince over his posterity to reign eternally in that position. Jesus Christ will be officially received as King of kings, and Lord of lords. . . . "Christ is the Great High Priest; Adam next," and according to the Prophet Joseph Smith, Noah or Gabriel "stands next to Adam in the Priesthood." In fact, each great prophet who held keys of the Priesthood over a dispensation will continue to hold that same authority and blessing. Thus Joseph Smith will retain his position as the head of the Dispensation of the Fullness of Times.

Man, by himself, could not know anything about God, except as God has revealed Himself. *God has revealed Himself in creation* (in nature), *The heavens declare the glory of God; and the firmament showeth his handiwork* (Psalm 19:1). *God has revealed Himself* and His commands *by means of man's conscience* (II Corinthians 1:12, II Corinthians 4:2, and other Scripture).

Then, *God saw fit to reveal Himself by the Living Word* (The Lord Jesus Christ, John 1:14 and Hebrews 1:1-3).

Lastly, *God has revealed Himself by the Written Word* (the Bible) of which the Lord Himself said, *Verily I say unto you, Till heaven and earth pass, one jot or one tittle shall in no wise pass from the law, till all be fulfilled* (Matt. 5:18).

It is difficult to comprehend how anyone would be willing to accept any humanized concept of God in the light of the glorious Scriptures.

WHAT DO THE MORMONS BELIEVE ABOUT JESUS CHRIST?

(1) *They do not believe that Jesus Christ was born of a virgin.*

Brigham Young taught that Jesus was the son of Mary and Adam, "When the Virgin Mary conceived the child, Jesus, the Father had begotten him in his own likeness. He was not begotten by the Holy Ghost. And who is his Father? He is the first of the human family;. . ." (*Journal of Discourses,* Vol. 1, p. 50). Brigham Young also stated, "Now remember from this time forth, and forever, that Jesus Christ was not begotten by the Holy Ghost" (*Journal of Discourses*, Vol. 1, p. 51). This statement was in conflict with both the Bible and the *Book of Mormon.* Nevertheless, the late Joseph Fielding Smith denied that the *Book of Mormon* and the Bible teach that Christ was begotten by the Holy Ghost. "They tell us that the *Book of Mormon* states that Jesus was begotten of the Holy Ghost. I CHALLENGE THAT STATEMENT. The *Book of Mormon* teaches NO SUCH THING! NEITHER DOES THE BIBLE" (*Doctrines of Salvation*, Vol. 1, p. 19; emphasis ours). The late Joseph Fielding Smith made this statement, "Christ was begotten of God. He was not born without the aid of man, and that man was God" (*Doctrines of Salvation*, Vol. 1, p. 18).

Brigham Young's opinion was, "The birth of the Savior was as natural as are the births of our children; it was the result of natural action. He partook of flesh and blood—was begotten of his Father, as we were of our fathers" (*Journal of Discourses*, Vol. 8, p. 115).

Heber C. Kimball, as a member of the First Presidency of the Mormon Church stated, "In relation to the way in which I look upon the works of God and his creatures, I will say that I was naturally begotten; so was my father, and also my Savior Jesus Christ" (*Journal of Discourses*, Vol. 8, p. 211).

In statements too numerous to quote, Mormon leaders have taught that Jesus Christ was not begotten by the Holy Ghost, that Mary was the wife of Joseph and another husband, that Mary and God the Father "associated together in the capacity of husband and wife."

Matthew 1:18 and 20 reads, *Now the birth of Jesus Christ was on this wise: When as his mother Mary was espoused to Joseph, before*

they came together, she was found with child of the Holy Ghost. . . .
For that which is conceived in her is of the Holy Ghost. "

The repudiation of the virgin birth is necessarily the setting aside of the whole system of Christianity, whether regarded as a body of Divine doctrine or as a revelation of saving grace to man.

When the Angel Gabriel came to Joseph, to allay his suspicions concerning Mary's state, and the Babe she was about to bear, he authorized Joseph to take her to himself, to fully receive her, and he spoke of her as, "Mary, thy wife."

That Joseph was *not* the father of her Child is self-evident, for when he found she was about to become a mother he determined to "put her away," that is, he would divorce her. But he was not willing to do this publicly because he would have to bring her before the elders of the congregation. Then she would be tried. Should the judges find her guilty, they would condemn her to be stoned to death. She would be taken outside the town into an open place; her accusation would be proclaimed by a herald and then the people would take up stones and stone her until she died. Joseph shrank from that. He loved her. He loved her even though he believed her to be unfaithful to him. The account in the Scriptures of Joseph's attitude toward the Babe proves that Joseph was not the father of the Child Jesus.

The denial of the virgin birth demonstrates that if Joseph were not the father, some other man must be. If some other man than Joseph were the father, Mary would be guilty of both faithlessness and personal unchastity.

If Jesus, the son of Mary, were begotten of a human father, as that father would inherit sin and be under the sentence of death upon sin, his son Jesus would inherit sin from his father and likewise be under the sentence of death. He would need, as all born in sin need, a personal Savior. If not virgin born, Jesus would need a Savior as much as any other man.

If not virgin born, Jesus would, as do all men, need to be born again. For if Christ were the son of a finite person, then He would also have a finite personality. If He had a finite personality he would not be an Infinite Person. If He was not an Infinite Person He would not be God. He would not be the Second Person of the Godhead; and if He were not the Second Person of the Godhead no one was. And if no one was, there would be no Trinity. But the Book we call the Bible teaches in a thousand ways, from Genesis to Revelation, that God is One Being; and in this undivided and indivisible Being, Three Distinct Persons perfectly and divinely exist.

The virgin birth is written into the Bible from the very first chapter.

In the third chapter of Genesis the Lord God announced to the woman that from her seed should come, the victor over Satan, sin and death. The victor was not to be of the *man's* seed, but "the seed of *the woman."* It *is an accepted fact that there is neither life nor potency for life in a* woman's seed; without contact with the male seed it cannot produce offspring.

When God stated that the Redeemer and Deliverer should come from the woman's seed He openly, clearly, and divinely proclaimed that Christ should be conceived and brought to birth without contact with the man's seed, without a human father.

In Isaiah 7:14, we read:

> Behold, a virgin shall conceive, and bear a son, and shall call his name Immanuel.

And the book of Matthew, written centuries later, announces the birth of Christ and declares it to be the fulfillment of the prophecy of Isaiah:

> Now all this was done, that it might be fulfilled which was spoken of [by] the Lord by [to] the prophet, saying, Behold, a virgin shall be with child, and shall bring forth a son, and they shall call his name Emmanuel, which being interpreted is, God with us (Matthew 1:22,23).

Luke gives the details concerning the birth of Jesus Christ in unmistakeable terms, stating that Mary was virgin when the Angel Gabriel announced to her that God had chosen her to be the mother of His Child. . .in the flesh (Luke 1:26-31). With all the simplicity, innocence and purity of her soul she said, *"How shall this be, seeing I know not a man"* (Luke 1:34). It is a perfectly clear statement that at that moment she was absolutely virgin, nor could she comprehend how, without the aid of man, she could become a mother.

Gabriel then told her the *how, "The Holy Ghost shall come upon thee, and the power of the highest shall overshadow thee; therefore also that holy thing which shall be born of thee shall be called the Son of God."* This was a dogmatic statement made by no less than an angel of God, that the conception and birth of this Child should be an event in which man would have no part. Therefore, heaven announced the virgin birth of Jesus Christ as the directly and only begotten Son of God.

The denial of the virgin birth and of the Trinity is more than the denial of a theological doctrine, it is a blow to destroy God's plan of redemption through the death of Jesus Christ. It makes untrue and impossible this glorious statement, *How much more shall the blood of Christ, who through the eternal Spirit offered himself without spot to*

God, purge your conscience from dead works to serve the living God" (Hebrews 9:14).

(2) *They believe in more than one Redeemer.* Consistent with the Mormon belief in a multiplicity of gods is their belief in more than one Redeemer. Mormon literature and official books of doctrine often refer to the "Army of Redeemers." These "Redeemers" include everyone from the Priesthood to the members themselves. As preached by Delbert L. Stapley of the Council of Twelve, and quoted in the *Improvement Era* magazine (June, 1961, p. 417), "As sons and daughters of God, we are required to purify and perfect ourselves in righteousness; otherwise, we cannot be with him nor enjoy eternal lives and glory in his kingdom." Stress is laid by Mormon leaders upon men paying the penalty of their own sins. Where is there need of a Redeemer, a Savior, if we must accomplish our own salvation? Romans 6:23 makes clear that our salvation is a gift, *"For the wages of sin is death; but the gift of God is eternal life through Jesus Christ our Lord."* And Acts 4:12 states clearly, *"Neither is there salvation in any other: for there is none other name under heaven given among men, whereby we must be saved* [than that of Jesus Christ]*."*

ARTICLE II

We believe that men will be punished for their own sins, and not for Adam's transgression.

Those whose doctrines concerning God are in error also teach unscriptural doctrines concerning man and salvation.

Mormonism, in common with many heresies of our day, is in reality autosoteric (man being his own savior).

In Article Number Two we read, "We believe that men will be punished for their own sins, and not for Adam's transgression." The Mormon people fail to realize that it was by Adam's sin of disobedience that many were made sinners:

> For as by one man's disobedience many were made sinners, so by the obedience of one shall many be made righteous —Romans 5:19.

We read in Romans, Chapter 5, verse 12:

> Wherefore, as by one man sin entered into the world, and death by sin; and so death passed upon all men, for that all have sinned:

In order to learn the nature of Adam's sin and the consequences we read in the book of Genesis, Chapter 2, verses 7-9:

And the Lord God formed man of the dust of the ground, and breathed into his nostrils the breath of life; and man became a living soul.

And the Lord God planted a garden eastward in Eden; and there he put the man whom he had formed.

And out of the ground made the Lord God to grow every tree that is pleasant to the sight, and good for food; the tree of life also in the midst of the garden, and the tree of knowledge of good and evil.

And in verses 15-17 we read:

And the Lord God took the man, and put him into the garden of Eden to dress it and keep it.

And the Lord God commanded the man, saying, of every tree of the garden thou mayest freely eat:

But of the tree of the knowledge of good and evil, thou shalt not eat of it: for in the day that thou eatest thereof thou shalt surely die.

This is the test of obedience given to Adam and Eve. They were warned that if they disobeyed they were to die. Death is the judgment of God upon man's sin of disobedience which fell upon Adam, the federal head of the race, and thus upon the whole race of man.

In Genesis Chapter 3 we read how Satan was able to persuade Eve to disobey God, through the lying assertion that human will, apart from God's expressed Word, can bring self-gratification and exaltation:

Your eyes shall be opened, and ye shall be as gods, knowing good and evil (Gen. 3:5).

As we have read, this is the lie that is propagated by the Mormon leaders. Their people are told that those who hold the priesthood of the Mormon Church shall become gods.

Eve was deceived through Satan's subtlety but Adam was not deceived. He knew full well the consequence of his sin.

And Adam was not deceived, but the woman being deceived was in the transgression (I Tim. 2:14).

Adam chose to disobey God, to forsake fellowhsip with God, to continue fellowship with the woman—which was wilful disobedience.

The moment Adam disobeyed God he died spiritually; he began to die physically, having become mortal. Then he was consigned to eternal death unless he should be redeemed from it.

Having disobeyed God, Adam became possessed of a fallen nature, which is in itself spiritual death, and this nature was passed on to his posterity.

> *For as by one man's disobedience many were made sinners, so by the obedience of one shall many be made righteous* (Romans 5:19).

Paul is not declaring that all have sinned personally, but all of us sinned in Adam the federal head of the race. But the glory of redemption is also by One Man, Christ Jesus.

> *For if by one man's offence death reigned by one; much more they which receive abundance of grace and of the gift of righteousness shall reign in life by one, Jesus Christ* (Romans 5:17).

The expression "one man" appears in Romans 5:12, 15 and 17. We see that there are two men, each the federal head of a creation, before God. There was Adam, the first; and he failed. God sent Another, and He did not fail! *The first man is of the earth, earthy. The Second Man is the Lord from heaven* (I Cor. 15:47).

This is known as the principle of "representation." The Mormons (as well as others) fail to comprehend this principle of representation— that we, the race, positionally sinned in Adam and hence are constituted sinners because of our part in Adam's sin. The Scripture makes it emphatically clear that for any member of Adam's race to go to heaven, he would have to accept Christ as his Savior. Then a great metamorphosis takes place as he is translated from Adam into Christ—from *death* into *Life*.

The cross of Christ is the heart and center of God's redemptive program for the race. Because of Calvary, God is receiving all who come to Him by faith in Christ. He imputes the righteousness of Christ to all who accept His Son as Savior. In other words, God can vindicate His holiness and justify the sinner because sin has been atoned for. He is just and is the Justifier of him who believes in Jesus.

When talking with some of the Mormon people, in reference to their Second Article of Faith, I show them Psalm 51:5 as further proof that we are sinners before God.

> *Behold, I was shapen in iniquity; and in sin did my mother conceive me.*

They will laugh and say to me, "Our Church [Mormon] teaches us that we are gods in embryo, that we can become gods, that we are not earth worms crawling in the dust, begging God for His mercy." I then ask them, "Do you believe in the Standard Works of the Mormon Church?" "The *Bible*, the *Book of Mormon*, the *Doctrine and Covenants*, the *Pearl of Great Price?*" To which they answer, "Of course, of course!"

Then I turn to the *Pearl of Great Price*, and show them the "Book of Moses," Chapter 6, verse 55:

> And the Lord spake unto Adam, saying: Inasmuch as thy children are conceived in sin, even so when they begin to grow up, sin conceiveth in their hearts, and they taste the bitter, that they may know to prize the good.

Invariably they are astounded and perplexed because they have never noticed this verse before. Then I call their attention to verse 54 of the same chapter in "Book of Moses."

> Hence came the saying abroad among the people, that *the Son of God hath atoned for original guilt.* . . .

This is in direct contradiction to their Second Article of Faith. Here again is displayed the strange paradox of the Mormon doctrine, as stated in their authorized books, which differs diametrically from the sayings and writings of their revered leaders and teachers.

But the natural man receiveth not the things of the Spirit of God: for they are foolishness unto him: neither can he know them, because they are spiritually discerned (I Cor. 2:14).

ARTICLE III

We believe that through the Atonement of Christ all mankind may be saved, by obedience to the laws and ordinances of the Gospel.

Although at first this too appears plausible, and to some even Biblical, a more careful study reveals the "*may* be saved" which robs one of certainty, and the qualification, "by obedience to the laws and ordinances of the Gospel." What does this mean, "obedience to the laws and ordinances of the Gospel?"

Mormon sources reveal:

> The Gospel of Jesus Christ is called the plan of salvation. It is a system of rules by complying with which salvation may be gained (Perry, E. F., *The Scrapbook*).

And in the book *Articles of Faith*, by Apostle James E. Talmadge:

> The sectarian dogma of justification by faith alone has exercised an influence for evil since the early days of Christianity.

Then in Milton R. Hunter's book, *The Gospel Through the Ages,* given to me by the late George Albert Smith, President of the Mormon Church in the year 1946, which was written to the quorums of the Melchizedek Priesthood, the author says that the things God tells His children to do we term the "Gospel of Christ." He states that it is a plan, a philosophy, which when applied will make mankind more like the Heavenly Father. He also adds that the resurrection, or the bringing about of the immortality of man, was accomplished through the atonement of Jesus Christ; stating that all men who have ever lived "regardless of how wicked or how righteous their lives have been, or who ever will live in this mortal world, will be made recipients of this great gift of the Savior's; that is, they will be resurrected and blessed with immortal existence."

Hunter writes:

> Death was overcome or destroyed by the Savior of mankind, and the law of resurrection put into operation. Following the resurrection, men and women shall never again die a physical death. In the words of Elder Joseph Fielding Smith:

> "Immortality is the gift of God, through Jesus Christ, to all men; by which they come forth in the resurrection to die no more, whether they have obeyed Him or rebelled against Him. This great gift is theirs; even the wicked receive it through the grace of Jesus Christ, and shall have the privilege of living forever, but they will have to pay the price of their sins in torment with the devil before they are redeemed."—Joseph Fielding Smith, *The Way to Perfection* p. 329.

> Eternal life, however, is a special blessing granted to a relatively few people because of their obedience to the Gospel of Jesus Christ. The word of the Lord to His children is as follows: "If you keep my commandments and endure to the end you shall have eternal life, which is the greatest of all the gifts of God." "He that hath eternal life is rich." On another occasion the Lord explained both immortality and eternal life to the Prophet Joseph and definitely made it clear that they were entirely different things. He declared:
> "And thus did I, the Lord God, appoint unto man the days of his probation — that by his natural death he might be raised in

immortality unto eternal life, even as many as would believe; and they that believe not unto eternal damnation; for they cannot be redeemed from their spiritual fall, because they repent not."

Eternal life is the kind of life possessed by the Heavenly Father and His Only Begotten Son; therefore, those mortals who attain it shall dwell in the presence of the divine beings. In a revelation to the Church members, the Savior declared, "If thou wilt do good, yea, and hold out faithful to the end, thou shalt be saved in the kingdom of God, which is the greatest of all the gifts of God; for there is no gift greater than the gift of salvation — eternal life."

It is difficult to understand the writings of Milton R. Hunter, in which he declares that in order to have salvation we must keep all the laws and ordinances of the Gospel, and then on the other hand declares eternal life to be a *gift* of God. In other words, in order to be saved one must keep all the laws and ordinances as defined by the Mormon Church. One must not only keep part of the law, but "all" the law, according to Mormonism. Again, in defining eternal life, Mr. Hunter says, on page 11 of his book:

Eternal life is the condition of life that those who live righteous lives will enjoy throughout the ages in the Kingdom of God. In fact it means exaltation. He who receives the greatest portion of eternal life becomes a God.

If salvation were obtained by obedience to the laws and ordinances of the Gospel as defined by the Mormon Church, then very few Mormons would be in heaven, because they violate the first commandment as given to us in the Gospel of Mark 12:28-30:

And one of the scribes came, and having heard them reasoning together, and perceiving that he he had answered them well, asked him, Which is the first commandment of all?
And Jesus answered him, The first of all the commandments is, Hear O Israel; the Lord our God is one Lord: And thou shalt love the Lord thy God with all thy heart, and with all thy soul, and with all thy mind, and with all thy strength. This is the first commandment.

The Mormons, with their doctrine of many gods would therefore, fail to qualify as recipients of eternal life. They do not believe in the *one Lord* of the Bible.

The Bible clearly states that salvation is not by works but by grace, through faith in the Lord Jesus Christ, and not by the law:

> *Is the law then against the promises of God? God forbid: for if there had been a law given which could have given life, verily righteousness should have been by the law* (Galatians 3:21).

The words "atonement," "faith" and "salvation" are used in Mormon teaching, but the Biblical doctrine of salvation by faith in the Lord Jesus Christ Who died, the just for the unjust, is buried under a glacial mass of laws and ordinances that must be kept in order that one may be saved. Submission and obedience to the commandments of the church is the essential requisite of faith.

That wonderful text, Romans 10:9, *"If thou shalt confess with thy mouth the Lord Jesus, and shall believe in thine heart that God hath raised Him from the dead, thou shalt be saved,"* is explained in a recent Mormon tract as follows:

> In the first place this letter to the Romans was written to individuals who were already members of the church. They had rendered obedience to the laws of salvation and, having complied with those requirements, were entitled to salvation, providing their testimony remained with them like a living spring.

Could the Scriptural teaching of salvation by grace through faith (which is God's gift) be more plainly contradicted than this?

We remember that Mormons were even taught that their salvation hinged upon their belief in the revelation of polygamy. It is no wonder that their President Woodruff, who issued the Manifesto to do away with polygamy for expediency's sake, admittedly practiced it years after the Manifesto, having pledged allegiance to a "man" and his law:

> For behold, I reveal unto you a new and everlasting covenant. And if ye abide not that covenant, then are ye damned. . . .For no one can reject this covenant and be permitted to enter into my glory. *Doctrine and Covenant* Section 132.

The leader of the Mormon people must acknowledge the church's requirement for salvation.

In such distortions of the Gospel of salvation the Mormon Church is guilty of adding to and taking away from the Word of God, and we urge all Mormons to pray and ponder over Revelation 22:19.

In Romans, chapter four, the apostle, speaking of Abraham says,

"If Abraham were justified by works, he hath whereof to glory, but not before God. For what saith the scripture? Abraham believed God, and it was counted unto him for righteousness." It does not say that his works counted for righteousness, but his *faith*, adding the glorious Good News:

> *But to him that worketh not, but believeth on Him that justifieth the ungodly, his faith is counted for righteousness.*

To work is ingrained within man's natural impulses. He sees the whole realm of nature at work and he finds it difficult to absorb with his human understanding that the gift from heaven is to be without effort on his part. To believe this deflates his ego, and discourages his self-righteousness. Nothing left for him to do but believe? This seems altogether too easy for him, even foolishness. His pride and his self esteem are wounded when he realizes that God does not attach more value to his works.

The Bible says, *"How shall we escape if we neglect so great salvation."*

Man's great obstacle is not neglect of the subject of salvation— but his attitude of attempting his own salvation, neglecting God's way of salvation. It is not our sins which will condemn us — Christ has redeemed us from our sins. It is our lack of faith, our failure to *believe* what God has said is true, that there is none righteous "no, not one."

We see the two types of men, throughout all Scripture, throughout all history: The one in self-pride saying, "Well, I am not so bad after all. I am not as bad as many others. I do this and that that is good." And the other type of man who, without any defense of self, believes that the Word of God is true, that the Lord Jesus Christ can save, the man who cries:

> Oh, the love that drew salvation's plan!
> Oh, the grace that bro't it down to man!
> Oh, the mighty gulf that God did span
> At Calvary!
>
> Mercy there was great, and grace was free;
> Pardon there was multiplied to me;
> There my burdened soul found liberty,
> At Calvary.

There are two great words which especially characterize God's dealings with men, at the present time. The one is "grace" and the other is "faith." Grace from God toward man, and faith from man toward God—grace on God's part and faith on ours. Grace and faith belong together. One is the complement of the other. For by grace are ye saved, through faith. . . .

This is the age of grace, not the age of law. The law was given to Israel, along with the covenants and the priesthood. But with the resurrection of our Lord we were redeemed from the curse of the law (Galatians 3:13). And if man chooses to live today as under the law, he must remember that the Bible says: *Whoever shall keep the whole law, and yet offend in one point, he is guilty of all* (James 2:10).

It is on this subject that many have wondered why the Mormons are not consistent with the law by keeping the Sabbath and worshiping on the seventh day. There are many requirements of the laws of Israel which Mormons fail to perform.

I have long had a deep understanding of the heart's desire of the Apostle Paul, who, after he was saved and delivered from the law, longed to preach to his own people after the flesh, Israel. I, too, long to reach the Mormon people who are still under the bondage of the law and the priesthood. They seek to be justified by obedience to the laws and ordinances of the Mormon gospel. And, as our Lord said to the religious people of His day, "Except your righteousness shall exceed the righteousness of the scribes and Pharisees, ye shall in no case enter the kingdom of heaven."

Making this application today, what chance does the average Mormon person have? If their righteousness does not exceed the righteousness of their leaders they will never enter into heaven—why? The answer is that their leaders know not that Jesus Christ settled the sin question at the cross. They believe and teach that something *more* must be performed; *more to be done* before God will forgive them. When we tell them that God is demanding no good works at all, no religious observances or church ordinances, no duties, no sinlessness (except the perfect sinlessness of Christ, imputed to them by faith), some are astonished, many disbelieving, but some, where the Seed falls on the good ground of faith, *believe*. Praise God! And the law which shuts man out has been overcome by the grace which draws man in to favor with God.

It is true that God demands perfection before any member of the human race can enter into heaven and abide in His presence. But what God demands He has provided, in the Person of His Son, the Lord Jesus Christ, who knew no sin, but was made sin for us. When the Apostle Paul, a religious Pharisee, discovered this he could write that wonderful heart-cry to all Israelitish people of his day and ours, and I echo every word:

> *Brethren, my heart's desire and prayer to God for Israel is, that they might be saved.*
> *For I bear them record that they have a zeal of God, but not according to knowledge.*
> *For they being ignorant of God's righteousness, and going about to establish their own righteousness, have not submitted themselves unto the righteousness of God.*
> *For Christ is the end of the law for righteousness to everyone that believeth* (Romans 10:1-4).

ARTICLE IV

We believe that the first principles and ordinances of the Gospel are: first, faith in the Lord Jesus Christ; second, Repentance; third: Baptism by immersion for the remission of sins; fourth: Laying on of hands for the gift of the Holy Ghost.

The Mormons claim to be preaching a "restored gospel." "To restore" means to bring back to, or put back into the form of the original state.

What, exactly, is the "gospel"? Many, so-called "gospels" are preached today which are so different from each other that obviously all of them could not be right. In Galatians, Chapter 1, verses 8 and 9, a double curse of God is pronounced upon any man, or even an angel of God, who preaches "another gospel."

We do not have to guess about this matter. The answer is clearly given to us in the Bible.

> *Moreover, brethren, I declare unto you the gospel which I preached unto you, which also ye have received, and wherein ye stand;*
> *By which also ye are saved, if ye keep in memory what I preached unto you, unless ye have believed in vain.*
> *For I delivered unto you first of all that which I also received, how that Christ died for our sins according to the scriptures;*
> *And that he was buried, and that he rose again the third day according to the scriptures* (I Corinthians 15:1-4).

The Gospel, then, is the Good News concerning the death and resurrection of Jesus Christ from the dead. The word "Gospel" is *evangellum*, translated in the Greek, and means "the good news message." The word as such is never found in the Old Testament. It is the "good news" that while God condemns us, Jesus came to pay the penalty of our sins and rose to provide a righteousness for all eternity.

The Bible says that Christ died for our sins, according to the Scriptures, and that He was buried, and that He rose again the third day, according to the Scriptures.

With all that has been written heretofore, we have seen that the "Restored Gospel" has nothing in common with the Gospel which the Apostle Paul preached. The Mormon gospel is not a "restored" gospel, as claimed, but "another gospel." The only way by which any man can decide if a religious system is of God or is of Satan is by comparing its teachings with the Word of God. And this we can only perceive by studying the system in the light of the Bible, and not the Bible in the light of the religious system, or false principle.

In Isaiah 8:20 we read:

To the law and to the testimony: if they speak not according to this word, it is because there is no light in them.

And in Proverbs 14:12:
There is a way which seemeth right unto a man, but the end thereof are the ways of death.

In John 14:6, we hear our Lord saying:
I am the way, the truth, and the life: no man cometh unto the Father, but by me.

If Christ *is* the only way, then all other ways are blocked.

God has provided mercy in His Son Jesus Christ, who came to seek and to save that which is lost.

But if our gospel be hid; it is hid to them that are lost: In whom the god of this world hath blinded the minds of them which believe not, lest the light of the glorious gospel of Christ, who is the image of God, should shine unto them (II Corinthians 4:3,4).

The god of this world, Satan, is the Great Counterfeiter, the master-mind behind all false religions.

In this age of grace, Satan wants people to be religious, kind, benevolent, to join churches, pay their tithes, and lead clean, respectable lives in their community. While this is all right for the

Christian, apart from Christ it becomes an embalming fluid or antiseptic to keep the world from smelling Adam's corpse.

The purpose of Satan, then, is to deceive men in relation to the truth of God. He would misrepresent God, His Person, His Work and His Word. The masses of mankind today are deluded by Satan in a deception that is both tragic and pitiful. They are blinded by his treachery and fraud.

The success of a counterfeiter, it has been said, depends largely upon how closely the counterfeit resembles the genuine article. Heresy is not so much the total denial of truth, as a perversion of it. This is why a half-lie is always more dangerous than a complete repudiation. When the Father of Lies sends out his emissaries, it is not their custom to flatly deny the fundamental truths of Christianity. Rather, they will tacitly acknowledge them and then proceed to give an erroneous interpretation and a false application.

For example, the devil would not be so foolish as to boldly announce his disbelief in a personal God. He takes His existence for granted and then gives a false description of God's character.

The whole world (apart from Christ) is lost; but the world does not know it. And the devil's business is to keep the people of the world ignorant of their condition. The millions in America who are not saved do not realize they are lost. They have, in some way, been lulled to sleep; their consciences quieted. This is the devil's business. He is blinding their minds, lest the Gospel of the grace of God should shine upon them, bringing Light to their darkened souls.

Sin has created spiritual disorder in the life of every person. The most insidious aspect of sin's affliction is a spiritual blackout, produced in the minds of the unsaved. When man's ability to understand the things of God is darkened, he will not accept the revelation of God's Word, but he likes to follow the high-sounding wisdom of men. Men reinforce themselves with their own feeble reasonings, plunging their minds still deeper into darkness. They are "ever learning and never able to come to the knowledge of Truth." This spiritual darkness is so subtle that while the unsaved scorns the light he thinks himself very practical, wise and judicious, well balanced and mature. His so-called common sense, pride and self-sufficiency have blinded him to his darkened spiritual state and indescribable danger. And back of this deep-seated spiritual ignorance is the skillful working of the god of this world, the devil, who is concentrating his clever deceit on keeping men from responding to the enlightening Truth of the Gospel of Christ. He persistently tells them that "all is well," "no need to be alarmed." And thus the Gospel is obscured in the minds of those who need it most, the spiritually dead.

In a measure, the Church is responsible for the rapid growth of today's false religions. In some circles there is a dearth of doctrinal teaching and preaching from the pulpits, and the result is that some members of the Church are enticed from the fold through the representatives of these false religions. Ministers of the Gospel would do well to indoctrinate their people. When the Church fails to declare the whole counsel of God, some part of the system of truth is neglected. Satan, then, grasps this opportunity to entice uninstructed people away from the fold. Truth is being sacrificed on the altar of courtesy. The desire not to offend, evidenced by so many ministers of the Gospel, has deterred them from drawing sharp lines of distinction between false doctrines and the truth. Compromising terminology would hardly fit into the usage of the New Testament writers, who vigorously contended "for the faith which was once delivered unto the saints."

Reading from II Corinthians 11:13-15, we learn:

For such are false apostles, deceitful workers, transforming themselves into the apostles of Christ.

And no marvel; for Satan himself is transformed into an angel of light.

Therefore it is no great thing if his ministers also be transformed as the ministers of righteousness; whose end shall be according to their works.

Let us notice, the expression in verse 13, "false apostles."

A few years ago, when I was waiting for my interview with the late President of the Mormon Church, George Albert Smith, I was told to return to his office in thirty minutes. I therefore went out on the street corner and noticed a company of young people who were waiting for the guide to take them on a tour through Brigham Young's home. I decided to accompany the group, hoping that I might have an opportunity to witness for Christ.

When we were about half way through the tour, our guide said something about our wonderful heritage as Mormons, and that we should be very grateful to God for the opportunity to be raised in the "true faith." Then the guide added that another mark of the true Church of Jesus Christ of Latter Day Saints, known as Mormons, is that they are the only organization which has the twelve apostles, saying, "Did not Christ have twelve apostles? Of course. Well, no other church organization has. The Mormons are the only religious group that has the twelve—the same organization that Christ had when He was on this earth."

At this point I raised my hand and said, "May I ask a question?"

"Of course," came the reply, "What is your question?"

I said that the Bible tells us that there are false apostles as well as true apostles, and I asked, "What then are the credentials of the true apostle? In other words, how are we able to discern between that which is true and that which is false?"

The guide's reply was, "I don't know."

I hastened, "May I answer my own question?" And I continued, "The reason there is no such thing as apostolic succession among the Christians in the Church is because, in order to be a true apostle of Christ one had to be an eye-witness to the resurrection of Jesus Christ from the dead, which is very plainly stated in the book of Acts, Chapter One" And therefore the only apostles that are functioning today are false apostles." (II Corinthians 11:13).

This broke up our discussion. I gave the group some gospel tracts and proceeded to my interview with President George Albert Smith.

We read in Acts 1:20-25:

For it is written in the book of Psalms, Let his habitation [Judas'] be desolate, and let no man dwell therein: and his bishoprick let another take.

Wherefore of these men which have companied with us all the time that the Lord Jesus went in and out among us,

Beginning from the baptism of John, unto that same day that he was taken up from us, must one be ordained to be a witness with us of his resurrection.

And they appointed two, Joseph called Barnabas, who was surnamed Justus, and Matthias.

And they prayed, and said, Thou, Lord, which knowest the hearts of all men, shew whether of these two thou hast chosen,

That he may take part of this ministry and apostleship, from which Judas by transgression fell, that he might go to his own place.

The Apostle Peter here reminds the other disciples that Judas had gone "to his own place," that he had been numbered with the others and had obtained part of this ministry. He states that it is now necessary that one should be appointed to take the place of Judas. And, in verse 21, "Wherefore of these men which have companied with us all the time that the Lord Jesus went in and out among us, beginning from the baptism of John, unto that same day that he was taken up from us, *must one be ordained to be a witness with us of his resurrection.*"

So, in order to qualify as an apostle of Christ, to be numbered among the Twelve, they had to accompany Him in His earthly ministry, beginning with the baptism of John, and also to be an eyewitness of His resurrection. Several qualified to become an apostle, but in order to choose the right one they cast their lots and prayed and God chose Matthias to take Judas' place.

Some may ask the question, "What about the Apostle Paul?"

Let us read what Paul has to say about this, in his first letter to the Corinthians, Chapter 9 verse 1. There were some at Corinth who questioned Paul's authority, so he said:

Am I not an apostle? am I not free? have I not seen Jesus Christ our Lord?

We see that Paul qualified to be an "apostle." He was a special apostle to the Gentiles. He was not numbered with the Twelve, but he did *see* the Lord Jesus Christ, in His resurrection glory, on the road to Damascus.

"True apostolic succession" is being built upon the foundation given in I Corinthians 3:10,11.

According to the grace of God which is given unto me, as a wise masterbuilder, I have laid the foundation, and another buildeth thereon. But let every man take heed how he buildeth thereupon.

For other foundation can no man lay than that is laid, which is Jesus Christ.

Satan, as we have discussed, wishes people to be religious.

And no marvel: for Satan himself is transformed into an angel of light (II Corinthians 11:14).

He wants them to be engrossed in religious organizations and rites. In fact, he is an advocate of human righteousness. His cohorts will persuade people to join a church, be baptized, pay their tithe, lead moral lives, try to keep the commandments, observe the Golden Rule. . .all of these, as a way of salvation. For when the Gospel of Jesus Christ can be veiled, whether by man's righteousness or religious enterprise, Christ is left out. He is left out as surely as if He were ruled out, driven out, scourged, denied, rejected, or despised.

Therefore it is no great thing if his ministers also be transformed as the ministers of righteousness. . .(II Corinthians 11:15).

We notice that Paul does not say, "as the ministers of evil." There are those who accept the reality of the devil, but who limit the activities of him and his agents. They look upon him as the agent of rampant vice and sin. They associate him with all that is repulsive and brutal, all that is sickening and horrible, but there was never a greater mistake. He seeks to do his most subtle work not as a repulsive, unattractive person, but as an "angel of light." He seeks to become influential in men's lives by means of beauty and culture. His ministers, Paul tells us, are not the coarse and sickening agents of rank and repulsive wickedness. They are "ministers of righteousness."

ANOTHER GOSPEL

Galatians 1:6-9 is a strong indictment from God's Word of those who would preach "another gospel." The gospel the Apostle Paul preached is recorded in I Corinthians 15:3, 4, *How that Christ died for our sins according to the scriptures; And that he was buried, and that He rose again the third day, according to the scriptures*: No wonder God has pronounced a curse on those who would trifle with the precious saving Gospel of Christ.

The Apostle Paul had been saved out of the religion of Judaism. He had a burning desire to reach his own people with the Gospel. We read his words in Romans 10:1-3:

Brethren, my heart's desire and prayer to God for Israel is, that they might be saved. For I bear them record that they have a zeal of God, but not according to knowledge. For they being ignorant of God's righteousness, and going about to establish their own righteousness, have not submitted themselves unto the righteousness of God.

This is true of the Mormon people and we cannot express how we long to reach them with the true Gospel of Christ that some might be saved before it is eternally too late.

Men's great religious institutions are their most arrogant boast today, but it is evident that the Lord Jesus is not in their midst, but often stands outside the doors, beseeching men to come unto Him.

It is unthinkable to the religious leaders that they themselves could be lost sinners, needing to be born again. They drift along, sheltered in their church instead of in Christ, vainly trusting human leadership. To such blind folly Christ said, "The Publicans and harlots go into the kingdom before you."

ARTICLE V

We believe that a man must be called of God, by prophecy, and by the laying on of hands, by those who are in authority to preach the Gospel and administer in the ordinances thereof.

According to Mormonism, in the third or fourth century after Christ, the world rejected the message of the Gospel proclaimed by the twelve apostles, so, in due course of time, God withdrew the Gospel, priesthood and authority from the earth. It is their claim that the world then went into apostasy and there were thereafter no true representatives of God on earth. Therefore, the ordinances of the Gospel could not be administered acceptably to God, and all such ceremonies as were established among the various sects were of necessity void until Joseph Smith received his purported "revelation" from God.

We read, in Joseph Smith's testimony, that a messenger from heaven, John the Baptist, conferred upon Joseph Smith and Oliver Cowdery the priesthood. Hence, Joseph Smith and Oliver Cowdery received the keys of the kingdom which gave them the authority to act for Christ upon the earth and to organize His Kingdom in the latter days. The church, the priesthood and the authority were allegedly restored through the Prophet Joseph Smith.

The Mormons ask this question of those engaged in Christian work, "Where do you get your authority?"

Not only does Mormonism claim, as we have seen, to have the authority in spiritual matters, but also claims authority over the governments of this earth.

In Volume I, page 230 of the *Journal of Discourses*, John Taylor, President of the Mormon Church (April 8, 1853), said, "Let us now notice our political position in the world. We are going to possess the earth. Now, ye kings and emperors, help yourselves if you can, this is the truth. . . ."

J. M. Grant, giving an address in the Tabernacle at Salt Lake City, said, on February 19, 1854:

> If you maintain the fact that the priesthood of God is upon the earth, and God's representatives are upon the earth, the mouthpiece of Jehovah, the head of the kingdom of God upon the earth, and the will of God is done upon earth as it is in heaven, it follows that the government of God is upon the earth. I allude to the Church which it dictates and then to the whole earth which it will dictate. . . .They will then find out whether Joseph [Smith] had a right to rule this earth by the power of the priesthood.

In an address given by Brigham Young on February 18, 1855, in the Mormon Tabernacle, Salt Lake City, their prophet said:

> . . .there has not been a President, nor a Governor, in our day, but what has been controlled, more or less, by priests who deny revelation, believe not in visions and receive not the ministration of

angels. . .and when the Constitution of the United States hangs, as it were, upon a single thread, they will have to call for the Mormon Elders to save it from utter destruction, and they will step forth and do it.

It is no wonder, in view of such claims, that the Mormons ask of others the question, "Where do you get your authority?" To support their own argument they confidently quote Hebrews 5:4, *And no man taketh this authority [honor] unto himself, but he that is called of God, as was Aaron.* This very verse, however, condemns the Mormon priesthood. They are the ones who are guilty of taking this authority unto themselves, which we will endeavor to prove.

In the first place, the Levitical Priesthood (Aaronic) was never given to anyone except the nation of Israel and was confined to the house of Aaron and the tribe of Levi.

What advantage then hath the Jew? or what profit is there of circumcision (Romans 3:1)?

Who are the Israelites; to whom pertaineth the adoption, and the glory, and the covenants, and the giving of the law, and the service of God, and the promises;

Whose are the fathers, and of whom as concerning the flesh Christ came, who is over all, God blessed forever. Amen (Romans 9:4,5).

When the law was proposed, the promise to perfect obedience was that Israel should be unto God a kingdom of priests (Exodus 19:6). But Israel violated the law and God shut up the priestly office to the Aaronic family, appointing the tribe of Levi to minister to them, thus constituting the typical priesthood (Numbers 3:5-9).

Aaron and his sons were appointed priests of the most high God and the tribe of Levi was set apart from all other tribes to assist the house of Aaron in their priestly work. And to him and his house was granted the high privilege of drawing nigh as priests unto God.

A priest is one who is duly authorized to minister in sacred things, particularly to offer sacrifices at the altar and to act as mediator between men and God. Aaron, the head of the priestly order, was closely associated with the great lawgiver, Moses, and shared with him in the government and guidance of the nation. It was in virtue of the priestly functions that the chosen people were brought into near relations with God and kept therein. Through the ministrations of the priesthood, the people of Israel were instructed in the doctrine of sin and its expiation, in forgiveness and worship. In short, the priest was the indispensable source of religious knowledge for the people and the channel through whom spiritual life was communicated. Not only was the priesthood of divine institution, but the priest himself was divinely appointed thereto.

For every high priest taken from among men is ordained for men in things pertaining to God, that he may offer both gifts and sacrifices for sins. . . .
And no man taketh this honor unto himself, but he that is called of God, as was Aaron (Hebrews 5:1, 4).

Even our Great High Priest, Jesus Christ, came not into the world unsent. He received His commission and His authority from the Fountain of all Sovereignty. At the opening of His earthly ministry He said, "He anointed me". . . ."He sent me" (Luke 4:18). He came bearing heavenly credentials.

The high priest was to act for men in things pertaining to God, *To make propitiation for the sins of the people* (Hebrews 2:17).

The chief privilege of the priest, then, was access to God. He was to offer up sacrifices for sins, first in behalf of himself and then in behalf of the people. It was the chief duty of the priest to reconcile men to God by making atonement for their sins. And this he affected by means of sacrifice. He would be no priest who should have nothing to offer. Sacrifice is an integral part of the prerequisite of the priesthood. It was the high priest who went into the Holiest of Holies, behind the veil, in the Temple at Jerusalem, once every year, with an offering of blood which he offered first for himself and then for the sins of the people. This was done on the "Day of Atonement" (Leviticus 16:2-34; Hebrews 9:7).

The two great priests of the Old Testament were Melchizedek and Aaron. Of the two, Melchizedek was the greater. He was the type of Christ as high priest because he was a King priest (Genesis 14:18), and he was King of Salem. He had no recorded beginning of days, nor end of life (Hebrews 7:2-4). Hence, no earthly person held the Melchizedek priesthood. The Aaronic priesthood was often interrupted by death. The priesthood of Melchizedek was endless. Hence, Christ was made a priest after the order of Melchizedek.

In the institution of the office of the Priesthood the Lord's words to Moses were, *Take thou unto thee Aaron, thy brother, and his sons with him, from among the children of Israel, that he may minister unto me in the priest's office* (Exodus 28:1).

The priest's duties were strictly religious. They had no political power conferred upon them. Their services, their dependent position, and the way in which they were sustained, i.e., by the free gifts of the people, precluded them from exercising any undue influence in the affairs of the nation.

How vastly different this is from the Mormon priesthood, which, as I have mentioned, claims authority over the people and governments of this world.

When God gave the law and the Priesthood to the people of Israel, He also made eight great covenants; some were conditional and some were unconditional. God said to the people of Israel, "If ye walk in my statutes and keep my commandments, I will bless thee." His unconditional covenants were declarations as to what He was going to do regardless of the disobedience of Israel.

When Christ was born, the people of Israel were in covenant relationship to Jehovah. Christ came to confirm the promises made unto the fathers (Romans 15:8). But the people of Israel rejected their Messiah and a supernatural event took place while Christ was on the cross. The veil of the Temple was rent in twain, from the top to the bottom (Matthew 27:51).

In Hebrews 9:8 the writer states that the Holy Spirit is both the divine author of the Levitical system of worship and its interpreter. The first Tabernacle is the Holy Place. As long as that part of the Levitical institution was still in effect, Israel was to understand that the way into the Presence of God had not yet been opened. The division of the Tabernacle into the Holy Place and the Holy of Holies showed the limitations of the Levitical system and kept the people from coming directly to God.

When the new order of things was brought into being by the death of Christ on the cross, thus fulfilling the typical sacrifices, God rent the inner veil of the Temple, which separated the Holy Place from the Holy of Holies, making the two rooms one. This was God's object lesson to the Aaronic Priesthood that it's ministry was now over, that a new Priest had arisen after the order of Melchizedec. But Israel, in her apostasy, repaired the veil, and kept offering sacrifices until God in His wrath sent the Roman soldiers to destroy the Temple and scatter His chosen people throughout the ends of the Roman Empire.

The rending of that veil signified that a new and living way was to be opened through the cross. The whole Levitical order, with its priestly offerings, sacrifices and Temple worship, was a shadow and was now to pass away. Since the first covenant or testament could not do that which the New Testament (Christ's priesthood) could perform, it was set aside forever. But we call your attention to Hebrews 5:4 again, to remind you that the Mormons have resurrected that which God has done away with and have claimed this authority unto themselves. They are guilty of taking this authority unto themselves, and will be held accountable before the Judgment bar of God.

It was a serious matter to intrude into the office of the priesthood, unless one was called of God from the house of Aaron and tribe of Levi. God would bring instant judgment upon one who did. In Numbers 16 we read that some of the people of Israel with two hundred fifty princes of the assembly gathered themselves together against Moses and Aaron and questioned their authority. Moses answered them, "God will tomorrow show who He hath chosen to be in authority over the people of Israel." Korah and his company were speedily dealt with for the folly and sin of their rebellious movement. They had attempted to create a priestly order without divine authority. So Moses called upon God, and as the people were gathered before the door of the Tabernacle the Lord spake unto Moses and Aaron, saying, *Separate yourselves from among this congregation, that I may consume them. And God caused the earth to open her mouth and the ground did clave asunder and swallowed them up. And they went down alive into the pit and the earth closed upon them and they perished from among the congregation* (Numbers 16:21-34).

God, through Moses, appointed Aaron and his sons and the tribe of Levi to the priesthood. Once appointed they could not be supplanted or interfered with in the discharge of their duties. The priestly function was to be wholly free from interference on the part of the other tribes of Israel and also the civil rulers, whoever they were.

One of the greatest and best of the kings of Judah, Uzziah, was made to feel the instant judgment of God for this violation (II Chronicles 26:16-21). He transgressed against God when he went into the Temple to burn incense upon the altar. And Azariah, the High Priest, and other priests with him, rebuked Uzziah the king that he had sinned in taking this authority of the priesthood unto himself. Only the priests were consecrated for this office. They ordered him out of the Temple, but King Uzziah refused and became angry with the priests. God struck him with leprosy and he remained a leper until his death.

Here we see the seriousness of, and receive God's warning concerning, man's assuming the authority of the priesthood. We earnestly bring this to the attention of the Mormon people and their leaders.

When Christ ushers in the Kingdom Age, Israel will again become a Kingdom of Priests (I Peter 2:9; Revelation 5:10). The Jewish Temple and Tabernacle, however, were instituted for an entirely different purpose than that for which the Mormons use their temples. Jehovah instructed the people of Israel to build the Tabernacle, *That I may dwell among them* (Exodus 25:8; 29:45, 46). This was during their wilderness journey. Later this was supplanted by the Temple in Jerusalem. Then the transition from the outward to the final-and-abiding is marked by our Lord when He said, *Destroy this temple, and in three days I will raise it up* (John 2:19). By this declaration it is to be understood that His body had now become what the Temple had hitherto been. *For in Him dwelleth all the fulness of the Godhead bodily* (Colossians 2:9).

He appealed to His people to come to Him that they might have fellowship. Christ is saying that the Temple built with man's hands had served its purpose and was among the things which were to vanish away (Hebrews 9:24). Today, in this age of grace, God is not establishing his kingdom on earth, but building His Church. Judaism is no longer in view, with its temple worship, sacrifices and priesthood (Romans 11). God is not dwelling in temples made with hands (Acts 17:24), but His dwelling place is in the Church, the body of Christ (I Corinthians 6:19; Ephesians 2:16-22).

God said, as recorded in Exodus 19:5,6, *If you obey my voice indeed, and keep my covenant, then ye shall be a peculiar treasure unto me above all people: for all the earth is mine: and ye shall be unto me a kingdom of priests, and an holy nation.* This was a true promise and prophecy of and for Israel. But Israel failed to fulfill the condition necessary for national priesthood, as announced in Exodus 19:5.

Israel did not keep the covenant, hence, the conditional promise, "Ye shall be unto me a kingdom of priests," was not fulfilled. The tribe of Levi was substituted for the nation, and the national performance of that promise remains still in abeyance until Israel returns to her Lord. No group, in this day or any other, need imagine they can take Israel's place, and receive the same promise in her stead.

When Christ in the synagogue at Nazareth read from the prophecy of Isaiah (61:1,2), He confirmed this prophecy. Then He closed the book and stopped at the point where the prophecy had been fulfilled (Luke 4:18-20). "And the day of vengeance of our God" was omitted by our Lord because it was and is, still in the future. But when this is fulfilled, at His coming again, then it is declared of the nation of Israel, "Ye shall be named the priests of the Lord, and men shall call you the ministers of our God" (Isaiah 61:6; 66:21).

So, during this present age of grace, there is no priesthood, recognized by God on the earth. God has never recognized a priesthood except that which He ordained Himself, and confined to the nation of Israel (Exodus 19:6), and to the tribe of Levi (Exodus 29:9; Numbers 3). It is said, even of the Lord Jesus Christ Himself, that if He were on earth He would not be a priest. The reason given is that on earth priesthood belongs to the tribe of Levi only, and our Lord sprang out of Judah, of which tribe Moses spoke nothing concerning priesthood.

Christ is a Priest, but His priesthood belongs to heaven and not to earth. It is after the order of Melchizedek and not of the order of Aaron. The reason is recorded in Hebrews 7:23-28. The Aaronic Priesthood was interrupted by death, "But this man, Christ, because He continueth forever, hath an unchangeable priesthood."

Today Christ is the One and only Mediator (Priest) between God and man (I Timothy 2:5). He alone is our eternal high priest (Hebrews 7:24). He became both King and Priest after the order of Melchizedek when He offered Himself as a sacrifice for sin on the cross.

The Holy Ghost this signifying, that the way into the holiest of all was not yet made manifest, while as the first tabernacle was yet standing:

Which was a figure for the time then present, in which were offered both gifts and sacrifices, that could not make him that did the service perfect, as pertaining to the conscience;

Which stood only in meats and drinks, and divers washings, and carnal ordinances, imposed on them until the time of reformation.

But Christ being come an high priest of good things to come, by a greater and more perfect tabernacle, not made with hands, that is to say, not of this building. . .entered in once into the holy place, having obtained eternal redemption for us. . . .And for this cause he is the mediator of the new testament. . .(Hebrews 9:8-15).

Here God reminds us that the earthly Tabernacle was a figure for the time then present, and a prohibition against free entry into the Holiest was symbolic of the fact that the way into the true Holiest in heaven was not yet made manifest. Why? Because Christ's death for sin had not yet been accomplished. But now, the way into the very presence of God has been manifested through the death of Christ. Thus, the glorious message is now proclaimed (Hebrews 10:19-22).

The book of Hebrews, looking back upon the history of the people of Israel, sets forth the fact that the Levitical priesthood proved to be a failure in that it was incapable of securing victory over sin and full, everlasting communion with God. And so the author of Hebrews cites Psalm 110. The ideal priest must belong to the order of Melchizedek. Christ was the fulfillment of this prophecy, for He came out of Judah, a tribe with no connection with the Levitical Priesthood. While the claims of the old priesthood were based on genealogy, Christ's were displayed in His power of an endless life. The claim of Jesus to be the real fulfillment of the Psalmist's prophecy rested upon the fact of His resurrection and the proof which it afforded that His life was indestructible. The Psalmist had declared that the ideal high priest would be forever, and the only One, whose life could not be destroyed by death, to answer this requirement was Christ—a priest after the order of Melchizedek (*Zondervan Bible Dictionary*).

The Mormon priesthood, or any other earthly priesthood, would rob us of these precious truths and would set aside the Cross and the Resurrection, seeking to bring us under the bondage of men. As one has already remarked: "Nowhere in the New Testament is the Christian ministry described in terms of priesthood. Not only do the sacred writers refrain from calling the ministers priests, they deliberately do so. The Greek word for a sacrificing priest, "Hiereus," is never given to any minister of the Christian Church. Priesthood ignores the free activity of the Holy Spirit in the life of the Christian and the breadth of the diversity of His operations. *Where the Spirit of the Lord is there is liberty* (II Corinthians 3:17). A man-made priesthood permits no such liberty. It ignores the Holy Spirit and imprisons the people within a cast-iron system which is far more akin to the bondage of the Law than the freedom of the Gospel."

Stand fast therefore in the liberty wherewith Christ hath made us free, and be not entangled again with the yoke of bondage (Galatians 5:1).

Where once the Law and the Priesthood barred the sinner from coming directly to God, because of the sacrifice of Christ on the Cross we can now come boldly into the Holiest by the blood of Christ. This is the new and living way which God has made available to all who will come. Dr. Donald G. Barnhouse has said: "What a blasphemy for any religion to re-establish a priesthood, a temple, and seek to set up barriers between a soul and God. Any time a human priesthood is introduced between man's soul and God there is the undoing of all that Christ has accomplished for us.

"Think of the religions of the world in the light of their manner of approach to God. Any religion which exalts man to a position where he stands between any soul and God, is clearly a man-made religion. Out of the fallen conscience of man has come every depraved form of worship, seeking to set up a man-made approach to God, generally at great material profit for those who control it."

As we examine the claims of the Mormon priesthood, we find that there is nothing to recommend it in the light of God's Word. It can be presented only by false claims and inconsistencies with Holy Writ. There is one item by which the Mormon priesthood has consistently followed the Jewish custom, and that is found in the duty of the priests outlined in Hebrews 7:5:

> *And verily they that are of the sons of Levi, who receive the office of the priesthood, have a commandment to take tithes of the people according to the law.* The Mormons excel in this duty of the priesthood. They most certainly are able to extract tithes from their people. If the Mormons wish to be consistent with the Old Testament priesthood there are many other practices which should be continued. Any Old Testament scholar can enumerate these, for their benefit. In fact, it is not surprising that the "blood atonement theory" was practiced at one time by the Mormon Church, nor would a continuance of the blood sacrifices of animals be inconsistent. There are many questions one could ask these followers-after-the-law.

One question we would ask the Mormons. "You claim that the Apostles of Christ held the priesthood. Where do you find this in the Bible?" Quite to the contrary, it was the priesthood which led the people of Israel in their apostasy in rejecting their King Messiah and the ministry of the twelve apostles.

It was the priests, along with the Sadducees and the Pharisees, who were the chief enemies of Christ.

They were displeased when Christ healed (Matthew 21:15).

It was the priesthood with the Sadducees and the Pharisees and the civil rulers who combined together to crucify our Lord. The priests with the Pharisees and the scribes consulted that they might take Jesus by subtlety and kill him (Matthew 26:3, 4).

The priests hired Judas to betray Jesus with thirty pieces of silver (Matthew 26:14-16).

It was the chief priests and elders who accused Jesus at His trial (Matthew 27:12). It was the chief priests who mocked Jesus as He suffered on the cross, saying, "He saved others, himself he cannot save" (Matthew 27:41-42).

When the apostles gave witness to the resurrection of Jesus Christ from the dead, it was the priests and the Sadducees who laid hands on the apostles and put them into prison (Acts 4:1-3). The ministry of the apostles was confirmed with many signs and wonders wrought among the people. They also healed the lame and the sick and cast out unclean spirits.

It was the high priest and the sadducees who were filled with indignation at these miracles performed by God through the apostles, and they put them in prison (Acts 5:12-18). It was the high priest who commanded them (the apostles) not to teach in the name of Jesus.

Peter and the other apostles answered and said, "We ought to *obey God rather than men.*"

By this we see that the power of God was not vested in the priesthood. The priesthood had degenerated (when Christ was born) to such a degree that it became the enemy of God, Christ and the apostles. Our answer to their question of us, "Where is your authority?" is this:

We are not priests. We are ministers, ambassadors for Christ. Our authority?

II Corinthians 5:18-20: *And all things are of God, who hath reconciled us to himself by Jesus Christ, and hath given to us the ministry of reconciliation;*

To wit, that God was in Christ, reconciling the world unto himself, not imputing their trespasses unto them; and hath committed unto us the word of reconciliation.

Now then we are ambassadors for Christ, as though God did beseech you by us: we pray you in Christ's stead, be ye reconciled to God.

ARTICLE VI and ARTICLE VII

6. *We believe in the same organization that existed in the Primitive Church, viz., apostles, prophets, pastors, teachers, evangelists, etc.*
7. *We believe in the gift of tongues, prophecy, revelation, visions, healing, interpretation of tongues, etc.*

The Mormon missionaries, approximately seventeen thousand at this writing, are making great strides in their proselyting work, claiming to represent the only "True Church on the earth." To an uninstructed person, Joseph Smith's story of having a revelation from God the Father and the Son, to restore the Church to earth once again, may be most convincing.

"THE SAME ORGANIZATION"?

When presenting Mormonism, the question is asked with delight by the missionaries, "Didn't Christ have an organization when He was here on earth?" To this many agree, and they proceed to say, "Your church (regardless of the denomination) is an incomplete organization. Where are your apostles? We are the only Church that has the twelve apostles, in essence the same organization that Christ had when He was here on earth." And this appeals to the logic of many listeners.

In order to give a proper answer to this, the Bible must be studied and interpreted in the light of the threefold division of the Word of God, as recorded in I Corinthians 10:32, *Give none offence, neither to the Jews, nor to the Gentiles, nor to the Church of God.*

We should all be familiar with the history and beginnings of these three distinct bodies of people. Before the cross of Calvary there were two classes of people on earth, Jews and Gentiles. Most of the Bible is concerned with God's dealings with the Jewish people.

The history of the Gentiles is contained in the first eleven chapters of the Book of Genesis, covering a period of approximately two thousand years. The history of the beginning of the Jewish race starts with the call of Abraham, as recorded in the twelfth chapter of Genesis, ending with the time of Christ and His death, burial and ascension into heaven.

We are now living in the Church Age, also known as the Age of Grace, in which God is building the Body of Christ out of the Gentile and Jewish races. The "middle wall of partition" (Ephesians 2:14) has now been broken down and there is no difference between Jew and Gentile. When Jew or Gentile hears the message of the gospel and responds by receiving Christ as Lord and Savior, through the operation of the Holy Spirit, he is placed into the Body of Christ, which is the Church.

There is neither Jew nor Greek, there is neither bond nor free, there is neither male nor female: for ye are all one in Christ Jesus (Galatians 3:28).

A few years ago the parents of a young Mormon who was to go on a mission for the church requested that I talk to him about the inconsistencies in the Mormon religion. The boy's parents had been converts to the Mormon Church, but had left the system after investigating the truth about Joseph Smith's history, in Washington, D. C. Several Mormon elders accompanied the young man to my home, at his request. Our talk began with some of the Articles of Faith of the Mormon Church, regarding baptism, authority, church organization and with special emphasis on their Article of Faith Number Six. They reminded me that the Mormon Church is the only organization which has the twelve apostles, and the same organization which Christ had when He was here on this earth.

Passing this argument by, I said, "Let us assume that you do have the same organization which Christ had when He was on earth. You should then, of course, be consistent and have the same message and program that Christ and the Twelve had when they were on this earth." And to this they agreed. Then I asked them to turn to Matthew 10, in order to test their argument with God's Word.

We read Matthew 10:1-10. I reminded them that in verse five Christ commanded His apostles not to go into the way of the Gentiles, nor to the Samaritans, but to go rather to the lost sheep of the house of Israel. I pointed out how inconsistent they are with this program, given by Christ, for most of their proselyting is among the Gentiles. I also reminded them that the message they preach is in reference to the kingdom of heaven being at hand, pointing out that there is no similarity between this and what Christ commissioned His Twelve to proclaim.

I then asked them to turn with me to Matthew 15:21-28: *And, behold, a woman of Canaan came out of the same coasts, and cried unto him saying, Have mercy on me, O Lord, thou son of David; my daughter is grievously vexed with a devil.*

But he answered her not a word. And his disciples came and besought him, saying, Send her away; for she crieth after us.

But he answered and said, I am not sent but unto the lost sheep of the house of Israel.

Then came she and worshipped him, saying, Lord, help me.

But he answered and said, It is not meet to take the children's bread, and cast it to dogs.

And she said, Truth, Lord; yet the dogs eat of the crumbs which fall from their masters' table.

Then Jesus answered and said unto her, O woman, great is thy faith; be it unto thee even as thou wilt. And her daughter was made whole from that very hour.

Here we have the story of the Syrophenician woman, a Gentile, who sought out the Lord Jesus Christ in behalf of her demon-possessed daughter. She cried unto Him, "Have mercy on me O Lord, thou Son of David. . . .But He answered her not a word."

I asked the Mormons, "Isn't this rather strange that the compassionate Christ would not so much as acknowledge the presence of this woman, who had faith to believe? In desperation she turned to the disciples of our Lord for help, but here again she was rebuked. They tried to get rid of her, and finally the disciples said to the Lord, 'Send her away. . .' And the Lord answered the disciples, not the woman, and said, 'I am not sent but unto the lost sheep of the house of Israel.'

"Isn't it strange that then she said, 'Lord, help me,' and He answered her. Why did He answer her, when He had refused to do so previously?"

The answer, is that she addressed Him as, "Lord, Thou Son of David," the first time, and as a Gentile she had no claim upon Him as the Son of David. But when she called Him "Lord" she received instant response."

"We notice." I explained, "that Christ said to her, 'It is not meet to take the children's bread and cast it to dogs.' She said, 'Truth, Lord,' for she knew her position as a Gentile, outside the commonwealth of Israel. But she was willing to take her rightful place, as a dog, begging for a crumb, and the Lord said, 'Great is thy faith.' And He granted her request and cast out the demon from her daughter."

Of course the Mormons had never been confronted with these passages of Scripture, and they wondered why the Lord had confined the ministry of the Twelve to Jews alone, and why He refused to acknowledge the Gentile woman.

This gave me the opportunity to show the Mormons, in answer to their confusion, that only the Jews were God's earthly covenant people and unto them alone were committed the oracles of God.

What advantage then hath the Jew? or what profit is there of circumcision?

Much every way: chiefly, because that unto them were committed the oracles of God (Romans 3:1,2).

We now know that the Jews rejected their Messiah and they are set aside temporarily, as recorded in Romans chapter 11.

As a result of the discussion with the Mormons in my home, the young man and his fiancée, who were about to embark as missionaries for the Mormon Church, renounced Mormonism. One of the Elders of the Mormon Church said to me, "If there has been a change from the earthly ministry of Christ and the apostles and we are no longer on Kingdom ground, then Mormonism is wrong."

For so is the will of God, that with well doing ye may put to silence the ignorance of foolish men (I Peter 2:15).

ALL OTHER CHURCHES ARE INCOMPLETE

The Mormon missionaries, in their proselyting work for their church, also say that all other churches are incomplete organizations because they do not have apostles and prophets. To support their position, they turn to the book of Ephesians 2:20:

And are built upon the foundation of the apostles and prophets. . . .

and Ephesians 4:11,12:

And he gave some, apostles; and some, prophets; and some, evangelists; and some, pastors and teachers;

For the perfecting of the saints, for the work of the ministry, for the edifying of the body of Christ:

The Mormons use these verses of Scripture to support the necessity of the church having apostles and prophets. However, these were revelatory gifts to the church at the beginning of the church age. When the written Word of God was complete these gifts were no longer necessary, so they were done away. (I Corinthians 13:8).

In I Thessalonians 2:13 we read that Paul gave special thanks that when he preached to the saints at Thessalonica they received his word as God's Word. You may ask, "What is so remarkable about that? Do not people do this today?" The answer to this is that there is a difference. Church members insist, and rightly so, that Pastors give the authority for their doctrinal statements from the Word of God. But this Paul could not do. He did not have a complete Bible. He was at that time writing the first of his epistles and he had previously visited Thessalonica. He had nothing on which to base his preaching except the Old Testament.

In that the Israelites had rejected their Messiah, both in incarnation and in resurrection, God raised up Paul and chose him as a special apostle to the Gentiles. He made known to Paul, by revelation, the truth concerning this Church Age. Obviously, when Paul told of God's revelation to him, there was no recorded Scripture to bear out his testimony. And so Paul would say that he "received this of the Lord," or "God revealed this to me."

In order to make Paul's preaching effectual God performed unique miracles for Paul and Barnabas, for in Acts 15:12 we read, *Then all the multitude kept silence, and gave audience to Barnabas and Paul, declaring what miracles and wonders God had wrought among the Gentiles by them.* And so we know that when Paul preached, God gave confirmation to the people's hearts by outward signs. In Acts 19:11-12 we read that God *wrought special miracles by the hands of Paul so that from his body were brought unto the sick handkerchiefs or aprons, and the diseases departed from them, and the evil spirits went out of them.*

Many Christians ask today, "Is the age of miracles past?" Or, "Why have we lost miracles today?" The answer is that in Paul's day there was need of miracles, because the early church had no written New Testament. When Paul preached, God gave him outward signs, as we read in Hebrews 2:4, *God also bearing them witness, both with signs and wonders, and with divers miracles, and gifts of the Holy Ghost, according to His own will.*

Paul could not show the people John 3:16, for this was not written until Paul had been in heaven for a long time. Paul could not turn to Ephesians 2:8,9. He had nothing in his hands. But Paul could say, "This is the word of the living God," and the house shook in which he was preaching. And many believed the message and were saved. *Now* the New Testament is written, the Bible is complete and we have no need for these miracles to confirm our ministry. Today's greatest miracle is the miracle of regeneration — man becoming a new creature in Christ.

LAYING THE FOUNDATION

In I Corinthians 3:9-11 we read on what foundation the Church was built.

> For we are labourers together with God: ye are God's husbandry, ye are God's building.
>
> According to the grace of God which is given unto me, as a wise master-builder, I have laid the foundation, and another buildeth thereon. But let every man take heed how he buildeth thereupon.
>
> For other foundation can no man lay than that is laid, which is Jesus Christ.

This is not the day of "laying the foundation." Paul laid the foundation and now the superstructure is being built. Since Paul's day, God has been building the Church, preparing it for Christ. Every member of the Church is to be "builded in" as a living stone.

We might use this as an illustration. When in Chicago I have been reminded that it, unlike New York City which is built on rock, is built on a mass of sand. Chicago is built on the shore of Lake Michigan, where it is said that fifty feet below ground water can be found. When skyscrapers are built in Chicago, builders dig down, about 50 feet and then, from there on down, they drive great piles as large as telephone poles. They drive as many as 50 in one place, all close together, and on top of these they put a solid block of concrete. Under these great buildings there are clusters of 50 pilings, close together, each covered with a great solid concrete foundation. And then they begin to build the superstructure.

Suppose that after ten stories of a building are built, a man comes along with a great load of piles for the foundation. The Master-Builder would say, "Take those back and bring us some steel girders, the foundation was laid long ago."

And so it is that today we do not need "Apostles and Prophets." Paul and his co-workers needed these, for, without the written Word, with only their spoken word, it was necessary that God testify to their witness by signs, wonders and miracles. And then Paul could say in conclusion, *I have laid the foundation; now you build.*

There is no authority today beside the written Word. If someone comes to you claiming he has a message from God, tell him you are satisfied with what is written in the Bible. Before the New Testament was written, the early Christians were prophesying. Being then without the Bible, God's written Word, God was revealing truths to them by this means, and Paul could write (I Thessalonians 5:20), *Despise not prophesying.*

The Holy Spirit came upon the people; sometimes they spoke in tongues; sometimes they prophesied. Those early messages were necessary at that time because there was no written message concerning this great new teaching, given by God, concerning the spiritual body of Christ — the Church.

When the time came that the New Testament was completed, prophesying and other ways by which God gave the early Christians messages of His truth, ceased. When members of the congregation received messages and prophesied, there was always the human danger of the people not receiving the truth. This left a wide open space for Satan to enter with his false messages. It was possible for a man to bring a message from Satan and say, "it was from God," so beautifully worded perhaps, that the early Christians might not have been able to discern the difference. This occurred in various places. Because of this, Paul had to reprove the people many times for certain teachings that had thus crept into the churches.

One of these instances is recorded in II Thessalonians 2:1,2:

Now we beseech you, brethren, by the coming of our Lord Jesus Christ, and by our gathering together unto Him, that ye be not soon shaken in mind, or be troubled, neither by spirit, nor by word, nor by letter as from us, as the day of Christ is at hand.

There were three ways in which false teachers could have come to this Thessalonian Church:

(1) *"By Spirit"* They had prophets in those days, men who stood up in the meeting and prophesied, led by the Holy Spirit. But the devil would counterfeit this. He sent false prophets among them to state the

truth, as Paul stated it, but adding something to it to blunt the edge of the truth and turn men away.

(2) *"By Preaching"* We have the full revelation of truth and we can turn to the Bible to get God's message of truth clearly.... They couldn't do that. A man would come into the assembly, stand up and preach, saying things that were not exactly true, as Paul said, "Nor by word" ... and that was *by preaching.* There were false preachers going about and some of them came into the gathering at Thessalonica.

(3) *"By Letter"* Then Paul wrote, "Nor by letter as from us" ... someone had written a letter and had signed Paul's name to it saying things in that letter that were not according to the truth. The people of that day were subject to that danger, but we have never been in that position. We have the full orbit of Christian doctrine recorded in the Bible by which we may check any man's preaching today.

Lacking this, Paul admonished them saying, *Be not turned aside, neither by Spirit nor by word nor by letter as from us as that the day of Christ* (Day of the Lord) *is at hand.* The original Greek rendering reads, *That the day of the Lord is now present.* Someone had said to the Thessalonians ... "The troubles that you are having are because of the man of sin, the anti-christ, who is dominating and who is sitting on the throne of Caesar. They were being taught that the end had come, that the day of the Lord was at hand, and this confused people.

A building can have only one foundation. The apostles and prophets who are a part of this foundation are those who labored with Paul during the transitional period, covered by the Book of Acts. Beside the Apostle Paul there were Barnabas (Acts 14:14), Apollos (I Corinthians 4:9), Silas (I Thessalonians 1:1; 2:6), Timothy (I Thessalonians 1:1; 2:6), Epaphroditus (Philippians 2:25), Titus (II Corinthians 8:23). Their number was seven.

The nature of their ministry was:

(1) Ministry of Reconciliation
(2) Ministry of Revelation
(3) Ministry of Perfection

(William B. Hallman's booklet, "The King and the Kingdom in History and Prophecy").

The Church, or those to whom the New Testament came, is said to be built on the foundation of the apostles and prophets (Ephesians 2:20), rather than that, the apostles and prophets were built on the Church. The Church did not bestow apostolic and prophetic authority upon *men,* but upon *chosen men,* moved of the Holy Spirit, who received and delivered the truth and doctrine by which the Church came to be. In the book of Hebrews, chapter 1, verses 1 and 2, we read, *God who at sundry times in divers manners spake in time past unto the fathers by the prophets, hath in these last days spoken unto us by his Son...*

Today, in this Age of Grace, God speaks to men through His written Word. In ages past, God spoke by the prophets (Hebrews 1:1) and at the close of the time of Law and the beginning of the Age of Grace, God spoke through His Son.

During the period covered by the Book of Acts and up to the time when the written Word was completed, God spoke to men through dreams, visions, signs and through prophesying.

During the beginning of the Church Age, some Christians had the special gift of prophecy and knowledge which was given to them by the Holy Spirit for the Church. But these gifts, necessary at one time, were to be withdrawn. Now that the revelation of God has been completed, now that all necessary prophecy has been made and God has recorded in His Word all He wants us to know of His plan and program, it is evident then, that there is now no need for anyone to have, or seek after, the gift of prophecy; nor is it necessary for God to speak to men in visions.

Today then, God speaks through His written Word, the Bible; hence, the admonition given to us in II Timothy 2:15, *Study to show thyself approved unto God, a workman that needeth not to be ashamed, rightly dividing the word of truth,* and in II Timothy 4:2, *Preach the word; be instant in season, out of season; reprove, rebuke, exhort with all longsuffering and doctrine,* and *Holding forth the word of life....* (Philippians 2:16).

During the transition period when God set Israel aside and made known by revelation to Paul the mystery concerning the Church, the early churches had need of prophets and apostles. Also signs and miracles were needed and given to confirm the preaching of God's ministers. This is the reason that we read in I Corinthians 13:8, *Charity never faileth: but whether there be prophecies, they shall fail, whether there be tongues, they shall cease, whether there be knowledge, it shall vanish away.*

This Scripture does not mean the prophecies would fail to come true, but the gift of prophecy, possessed by some at that time, would be withdrawn. Knowledge, then imparted in a supernatural manner, would cease to come by this means. They were part of the transition from an earthly program to a heavenly and spiritual one. It all hinges on two things — the setting aside of the Nation of Israel and the full revelation of Church truth. And so the Apostle wrote, *Whereof I am made a minister according to the dispensation of God which is given to me for you, to fulfill the word of God.* (Colossians 1:25).

There is no necessity for apostles or prophets in the Church today, for the Word of God is completed and in its written form is available to man.

There is no short cut to spirituality but to study the Word, pray and witness for Christ. The special gifts of apostles, prophets and visible signs were transitory, as J. B. Phillips wrote. "It is the invisible things that are really permanent."

ARTICLE VIII

We believe the Bible to be the word of God as far as it is translated correctly; we also believe the Book of Mormon to be the word of God.

Concerning the *Book of Mormon* Joseph Smith, on November 28, 1841, made this statement:

> . . .I told the brethren that the Book of Mormon was the most correct of any book on earth, and the keystone of our religion, and a man would get nearer to God by abiding by its precepts, than by any other book. (Recorded in *Teachings of the Prophet Joseph Smith*, p. 194.)

In his "Address on the Book of Mormon," President W. Arid MacDonald made this extraordinary statement concerning the *Book of Mormon*:

> . . .It is the only book in the world, out of all the millions of books in the libraries of the world, which was brought to the earth by an angel from the throne of God. That makes it different from all other books. The angel made fifteen trips to this planet from the throne of God to see that this book was properly translated and printed, so that it might be given to the world.

Mormon writer James E. Talmadge, in his book *The Vitality of Mormonism*, states unequivocally that Mormons make "no reservation respecting the *Book of Mormon* on the ground of incorrect translation," because to do so would be to "ignore attested fact as to the bringing forth of that book." He reiterates that Smith, the prophet, seer and revelator expressly declared the translation was effected through the power of God and "is in no sense the product of linguistic scholarship."

Among the many extraordinary claims of the Mormons concerning their wonder book, the *Book of Mormon*, are these, that it is:

(1) A book translated by the gift and power of God.

(2) A book with the uniquely unparalleled distinction of being a God-given book. (A distinction hitherto only claimed for the Bible.)

(3) That a miraculous device, called the Urim and Thummin, was supplied by God and delivered by an angel, to perform the super-natural wonder of translating the book from the unknown "Reformed Egyptian Hieroglyphics" into "modern tongue."

(4) That an angel was sent from the throne of God to make certain "That this book was properly translated and printed."

(5) That testimonies and revelations were given, after the book was translated and printed, that the work was from God and that it was genuine and true, and that it contained the "fulness of the everlasting gospel."

But, in spite of all the Mormon testimony to the genuineness and accuracy of the *Book of Mormon*, it is evident that more than three thousand changes have been made in the book which it is claimed was God-given, supernaturally translated, and angel-protected. There were major textual changes, as well as thousands of corrections in grammar, spelling, punctuation and capitalization. But all changes, regardless of how minor, should be disavowed and unauthorized if the 1830 Edition of the *Book of Mormon* is what Mormon leaders claim it to be.

It must also be remembered that this book is not thousands of years old, having been subjected to many translations, but the *one* translation of the *Book of Mormon*, supposed to have been executed by the power of God, was effected only a century and a half ago.

Some of the changes from the 1830 Edition have been previously referred to. On page 25 of the 1830 Edition we read:

"Behold, the virgin which thou seest is the mother of God."

In later editions this important statement is changed to read:

"Behold the virgin whom thou seest is the mother of the Son of God" (I Nephi 11:18).

Also on page 25, 1830 Edition, it reads:

"And the angel said unto me, behold the Lamb of God, yea even the Eternal Father!"

In the later editions it has been changed to read:

"And the angel said unto me: Behold the Lamb of God, yea, even *the Son of* the Eternal Father!" (I Nephi 11:21, Italics ours)

It is interesting to note that within pages 1 to 25 of the 1830 Original Edition of the *Book of Mormon*, when compared with later editions, more than five hundred changes are found to have been made.

Dr. Sidney B. Sperry, Professor of Old Testament Languages and Literature, at Brigham Young University, Provo, Utah, a recognized Mormon scholar, writes regarding Mosiah 2:16-18, in the *Book of Mormon*, "The homely English of this scripture could be much improved, particularly the first sentence."

In II Nephi 6:2, he says, "This is a very poor English sentence, parallels of which can be found many times over in the *Book of Mormon*" (*Our Book of Mormon*, pp. 79, 80).

Dr. Sperry explains the weaknesses in the *Book of Mormon* by calling attention to the fact that Joseph Smith was not an English scholar, that he lacked the experience and training to become a polished translator, even going so far as to say that "the Prophet lacked the skill of the King James translators."

This is unreasonable when we remember the manner in which the Prophet Joseph Smith is supposed to have translated the book. Said David Whitmer, one of the "three witnesses" to the *Book of Mormon's* origin:

> Joseph Smith would put the Seer Stone into a hat, and put his face in the hat, drawing it closely around his face to exclude the light; and in the darkness the spiritual light would shine. A piece of something resembling parchment would appear, and on that appeared the writing. One character at a time would appear, and under it was the interpretation in English. Brother Joseph would read off the English to Oliver Cowdery, who was the principle scribe, and when it was written down and repeated to Brother Joseph to see if it was correct, then it would disappear, and another character with the interpretation would appear. Thus the Book of Mormon was translated by the gift and power of God, and not by any power of man (Whitmer, David, *Translation of the Book of Mormon*).

In view of all this, Mormon churchmen admit no error in the prophet's story concerning the *Book of Mormon*, and while they persistently question the correctness of the Bible translation, (note opening clause of Article VIII) they concede no weakness or error in the *Book of Mormon*.

Scores of fully qualified students of literature, religion, history, anthropology, archeology and philology have examined the *Book of Mormon*, some critically but objectively, and have published their findings. Some have been forced to reject the book as a true source of information. The *Book of Mormon*, as a piece of literature, is insignificant and tasteless. It has been declared by many a mass of plagiarism and bad grammar. It contains no statement of philosophy or ethics except in those portions that have been borrowed from the Bible. Even the Mormons do not base their present-day teachings on it, and for that purpose it was supplanted within fifteen years of its publication by later writings of Joseph Smith (*Doctrine and Covenants* and *Pearl of Great Price*). It is a poorly presented mixture of Judaism and Christianity, lacking a clear statement of a means by which man may be redeemed.

The *Book of Mormon* is not the source of the doctrines of the Church of Jesus Christ of Latter Day Saints. It can scarcely be termed a book of doctrine, for doctrines are suggested, although not defined, and none of the peculiar beliefs by which the Mormons are distinguished today are present. For example, as we have mentioned, the Mormons teach "the sublime truth that God the Eternal Father was once a mortal man who passed through a school of earth life similar to that through which we are now passing." (Hunter, Milton R., *The Gospel Through the Ages*, Salt Lake City, 1945, p. 104.) And they teach that men through progression and exaltation may become gods in the same sense and with the same status as God the Father. (*King Follett Discourse*, Salt Lake City, 1955, p. 10.) But these and other doctrines which are the backbone of Mormonism today are absent from the *Book of Mormon*.

Another major doctrine of the Mormon gospel is the teaching of the church regarding "celestial marriage." We read, "The crowning gospel ordinance requisite for Godhood is celestial marriage. . . ." (Hunter, Milton R., *The Gospel Through the Ages*, pp. 118-120.) This "crowning gospel ordinance" cannot be found in the *Book of Mormon*.

No mention is made in the *Book of Mormon* concerning baptism for the dead, without which the multi-million dollar Mormon genealogical program, and at least two-thirds of their temple activity, would be meaningless.

The following reveals other "gospel" teaching of Mormonism that are not to be found in the *Book of Mormon*:

The Mormon church organization, with its rigid complexities, are not to be found in the *Book of Mormon*, although the church places great emphasis upon it.

The Mormon so-called "Melchizedek priesthood order" cannot be found in the *Book of Mormon*.

The Mormon so-called "Aaronic priesthood order" cannot be found in the *Book of Mormon*.

The Mormon doctrine of the plurality of Gods cannot be found in the *Book of Mormon*.

The Mormon doctrine of "the three degrees of glory" cannot be found in the *Book of Mormon*.

The Mormon doctrine of the plurality of wives cannot be found in the *Book of Mormon*.

The Mormon doctrine of "the Word of Wisdom" cannot be found in the *Book of Mormon*.

The Mormon doctrine of a "heavenly mother" cannot be found in the *Book of Mormon*.

If all the doctrines we have mentioned above were removed from the Mormon "gospel," the Mormon system as it is known today would cease to exist, yet not one of these vital tenets are found in the *Book of Mormon*, the "everlasting gospel in its fulness."

If the *Book of Mormon* had, in fact, contained the "everlasting gospel in its fulness," there would have been no need for the *Doctrine and Covenants*, the *Pearl of Great Price*, nor any "modern-day revelations" to be written, all of which have an intrinsic place in the Mormon system.

How then can Mormons claim that the *Book of Mormon* is a revelation of the "everlasting" gospel? How then are men to believe that it is "the most perfect book that was ever written"?

The problem which Mormons cannot explain is that if one is to believe Joseph Smith is the *Prophet of God* and the *Book of Mormon* the Word of God it is not possible, with any logic, to discredit one without discrediting the other.

The question arises of how thinking persons can accept the doctrinal omissions, fallacies, discrepancies, and inconsistencies of the *Book of Mormon* and its translator. The answer lies in the fact that the energetic program of Mormonism makes any danger remote of the average member studying the *Book of Mormon* carefully and arriving at the point of its incredibility.

No matter how far the *Book of Mormon* defies reason, fact, and the later revelations of their prophets, Mormons must believe that it was divinely revealed and divinely translated.

> This book must be either true or false. . . .If false, it is one of the most cunning, wicked, bold, deep-laid impositions ever palmed upon the world, calculated to deceive and ruin millions who will sincerely receive it as the word of God, and will suppose themselves securely built upon the rock of truth until they are plunged with their families into hopeless despair. The nature of the message in the Book of Mormon is such, that if true, no one can possibly be saved and reject it; if false, no one can possibly be saved and receive it. (Mormon Apostle Orson Pratt, *Divine Authenticity of the Book of Mormon*).

VIII

Wresting the Scriptures

False Interpretations

As also in all his [the Apostle Paul's] epistles, speaking in them of these things; in which are some things hard to be understood, which they that are unlearned and unstable wrest, as they do also the other scriptures, unto their own destruction.

Ye therefore, beloved, seeing ye know these things before, beware lest ye also, being led away with the error of the wicked, fall from your own stedfastness (II Peter 3:16,17).

Since the beginning of the Church Era, back in the days of the apostles, Satan's emissaries have been busy trying to discredit the Word of God. Or they use the Word of God with false interpretation, and, as Peter warns, "They wrest the scriptures to their own destruction."

The Mormons are guilty of doing this in their attempt to take seemingly difficult passages of Scripture, distorting their true meaning, to substantiate their false doctrines. One example of this is their erroneous interpretation of Ezekiel 37:15-17:

The word of the Lord came again unto me, saying, Moreover, thou son of man, take thee one stick, and write upon it, For Judah, and for the children of Israel his companions: then take another stick, and write upon it, For Joseph, the stick of Ephraim, and for all the house of Israel his companions: And join them one to another into one stick; and they shall become one in thine hand.

THE STICK OF JUDAH AND STICK OF EPHRAIM

Mormon teachers have the audacity to say that the stick of Judah is the Bible and that the stick of Joseph is the *Book of Mormon* claiming this as a fulfillment of prophecy. And thus, the Bible and the *Book of Mormon* have become "one in God's hand," according to Mormon

150

belief. It has always been a source of amazement to me that intelligent people can accept this erroneous interpretation, and yet Mormons have used this to advantage in their proselyting work. Many who are ignorant of the Scriptures are impressed by their presentation and application of this portion of the Scriptures and have been influenced to join the Mormon faith.

The central theme of Ezekiel, Chapters 34-37, is the regathering of the people of Israel back to their own land. The vision which God gave to the prophet Ezekiel of the Valley of Dry Bones, in chapter 37, represents the nation of Israel. The Israelites had been out of their land, had been buried among the Gentile nations, and were, in a sense, devoid of life. But God promised that He would bring His nation back to its land again.

At the time of this prophecy the nation of Israel was saying, *Our bones are dried up. . . .our hope is lost, we are cut off from the land.* But God, through Ezekiel, assured the people He would keep His covenant with Abraham and David. He would fulfill His Word to them (verses 11,12).

In verse 21 we have the explanation given to us again. So the first prophecy of Ezekiel 37 portrays the moral, national and physical resurrection of Israel, while the second prophecy (verses 15-28) predicts the future union of the twelve tribes and their restoration to Palestine under one Shepherd.

In I Kings, chapters 11 and 12, it is recorded that after King Solomon's death the nation of Israel was divided in two kingdoms. Only two of the tribes, Judah and Benjamin, were given to Rehoboam, Solomon's son, to rule over; while the other ten tribes were taken from him and placed under the leadership of Jeroboam, a servant in Solomon's house. This division persisted, and so, in the prophetic books of the Old Testament, the tribes, Judah and Benjamin, were designated as "Judah" and composed of the southern kingdom, while "Joseph," "Ephraim" and "Israel" were the collective names of the ten tribes who, under Jeroboam, established the northern kingdom. So, when Israel's history is studied, the prophecy under consideration becomes very clear. God promises, through the prophet Ezekiel, that He is going to unite the two kingdoms and make them one nation again, after He has gathered them back to Palestine, the land that He gave to their forefathers (See Ezekiel 37:21-15). It is then and there that He will make His covenant of peace with them, set His sanctuary in their midst, and be their God.

These "sticks" of Ezekiel 37 are simply the divine edicts of God which He gave to Ezekiel to deliver to the people. It is stated in verse

20, that these royal decrees, which Ezekiel was commanded to write, were to be in Ezekiel's hand before the eyes of the people. This was to show them that all twelve tribes would be united and become "one" in God's hand.

In the prophetic books of the Bible, Ephraim and Israel are the collective names of the Ten Tribes which under Jeroboam established the northern kingdom, subsequently called Samaria (I Kings 16:24). In 722 B.C. they were sent into an exile which still continues (II Kings 17:1-6). They were distinguished as the outcasts of Israel from the disbursed of Judah (Isaiah 11:12). They, with Judah, are yet to be restored to Palestine and made one nation again (Jeremiah 23:5-8).

Ephraim was the younger son of Joseph (Genesis 41:52; 48:14). In II Chronicles 17:2 we read of the cities of Ephraim. And in Judges 8:1 we read of the men of Ephraim. Ephraim could hardly refer to the *Book of Mormon.*

SAVING THE DEAD

We have previously discussed the practice, by Mormons, of baptizing for the dead, but we now examine this matter in the light of Scripture.

For Christ also hath once suffered for sins, the just for the unjust, that he might bring us to God, being put to death in the flesh, but quickened by the Spirit:

By which also he went and preached unto the spirits in prison;

Which sometime were disobedient, when once the longsuffering of God waited in the days of Noah, while the ark was a preparing, wherein few, that is, eight souls were saved by water.

The like figure whereunto even baptism doth also now save us (not the putting away of the filth of the flesh, but the answer of a good conscience toward God, by the resurrection of Jesus Christ:

Who is gone into heaven, and is on the right hand of God; angels and authorities and powers being made subject unto him (I Peter 3:18-22).

The true meaning of these passages of Scripture is distorted by the Mormon Church in its attempt to prove its doctrine of a second chance after death. Mormons tie this in with their practice of baptizing for the dead. They claim that all who have died without an opportunity to have heard of the Mormon gospel can be baptized, by proxy, and thus obtain salvation and progression, as do the living Mormon people now.

What is the scriptural meaning of these passages in I Peter 3?

In verse 18 we read how the Holy Spirit quickened the body of Christ in the tomb. This applies to His physical resurrection. In verses 19 and 20, He, that is the Spirit—the same Spirit who raised Christ from the dead—preached through Noah to the spirits in prison, which spirits were sometimes disobedient when once the long suffering of God waited in the days of Noah. So when the preaching occurred they were not in prison. They were the people who were living in the days of Noah. And the Spirit of God through Noah warned these generations of the coming judgment of God upon them. The time of the preaching, then, did not occur between the death and resurrection of Christ but it took place in Noah's day.

Christ was not personally or corporally present, just as He is not present in person in this age when the Gospel is preached. His Spirit is here. So was He present by His Spirit in the days of Noah. As it is written, *My spirit will not always strive with man, for that he also is flesh; yet his days shall be 120 years* (Genesis 6:3).

In long suffering, God was waiting for 120 years while the Ark was being prepared. His Spirit preached then through Noah. In him was the Spirit of Christ. He delivered the warning message of an impending judgment to those about him who did not heed the message, passed on into disobedience, were swept by the deluge and are now the spirits in prison (II Peter 2:5).

As the Spirit of Christ was in the prophets (I Peter 1:11), testifying beforehand of the suffering of Christ and the glory that should follow, so the Spirit of Christ preached through Noah.

This interpretation is in full keeping with Peter's testimony. It is to "strengthen his brethren" to encourage and comfort those who were suffering persecution and passing through many fiery trials. They thought it strange that they had to suffer, that they were few in number who were saved, while they lived in the midst of the vast multitudes which rejected the Gospel and lived on in sin and disobedience. For this reason the Spirit of God reminds them that such was also the case in the days of Noah, as it will be again at the close of the age, as the Lord Himself had announced. The multitudes in the days of Noah despised the warning; only eight souls were saved out of the judgment.

It must also be remembered that Peter's epistles are not doctrinal epistles; he does not teach but exhorts. And the theme of his epistles is that of suffering.

The sense of the passage here, therefore, is that, during the 120 years while the Ark was being built, the Spirit of God in Noah warned men of the coming flood. Only eight believed. The rest disbelieved and as a consequence were shut up in the prison of the abyss. The believers were sheltered in the refuge of the Ark and were saved through the waters of judgment in the baptism of the Ark. It suffered judgment, passed through it and rose out of it into the new earth. In the "anti-type baptism" the believer is saved in the baptism of Christ on the Cross of which the baptism of the Ark was a type. Christ at Calvary was baptized into the wrath of God. In His baptism the believer is saved and in His resurrection the believer is raised and brought into a new world.

For a further study on this interpretation of a seemingly difficult portion of Scripture (I Peter 3:18), we would refer our readers to the footnote of the *Pilgrim's Bible* on this passage. Also I suggest the *Numerical Bible,* published by Loizeaux Bros. Inc. (Nepture, N.J. Inc., 1903), beginning on page 159. For my own study I also used the Samuel Bagster & Son *Greek New Testament.*

We are warned in I Timothy 1:4, *Neither give heed to fables and endless genealogies, which minister questions, rather than godly edifying which is in faith; so do.* And we read in Titus 3:9, *But avoid foolish questions, and genealogies, and contentions, and strivings about the law; for they are unprofitable and vain.*

ELIJAH THE PROPHET

Again the Mormons are guilty of "wresting the scriptures," endeavoring to prove that the prophecy of Elijah, as recorded in Malachi 3 and 4, found its fulfillment in the prophecy allegedly given to Joseph Smith.

Behold, I will send you Elijah the prophet before the coming of the great and dreadful day of the Lord: And he shall turn the heart of the fathers to the children, and the heart of the children to their fathers, lest I come and smite the earth with a curse (Malachi 4:5,6).

Joseph Smith, the founder of Mormonism, made the claim, we remember, that an angel by the name of Moroni appeared to him with the message that God had a work for him to do. He said the angel informed him about a buried record, written upon gold plates, which he was to receive and translate by means that God had prepared. According to Joseph Smith's story, the angel then commenced quoting prophecies of the Old Testament, the first one being the passage we have cited about (Malachi 4:5,6). The Angel, however made some changes, according to Joseph Smith, and this is the way he quoted it:

Behold, I will reveal unto you the Priesthood, by the hand of Elijah the prophet, before the coming of the great and dreadful day of the Lord. And he shall plant in the hearts of the children the promise made to the fathers, and the hearts of the children shall turn to their fathers; if it were not so, the whole earth would be utterly wasted at his coming.

It is clearly seen that by thus adding to and misusing this portion of Scripture, the foundation is laid for the introduction of the complicated system of the Mormon "priesthood." Malachi's prophecy has been altered and distorted in order that this unfounded doctrine may be "proven" by the Bible.

As we examine Malachi's prophecy in the light of its context, we readily learn, from the opening verses of the book (*Malachi* 1:1), that this prophecy was given, not to the Gentiles, but to the nation of Israel. Malachi is the last of the Old Testament books, and since a long period of time was to elapse before the Lord would again speak to that nation, He sends Malachi to them with this message:

Behold, I will send my messenger, and he shall prepare the way before me (Malachi 3:1).

Then, in the closing verses of the prophecy, we find the passage in question, Malachi 4:5,6.

Now, when we turn to the Gospel according to Mark, we find the Spirit of God, quoting Malachi's prophecy and applying it to John the Baptist, who was the forerunner of Jesus Christ, the King Messiah.

As it is written in the prophets, Behold, I send my messenger before thy face, which shall prepare thy way before thee. The voice of one crying in the wilderness, Prepare ye the way of the Lord, make his paths straight (Mark 1:2,3).

In the Gospel of Luke we read of the angel who appeared to Zacharias, concerning the birth of his son, John the Baptist.

But the angel said unto him, Fear not, Zacharias: for thy prayer is heard; and thy wife Elisabeth shall bear thee a son, and thou shalt call his name John.

And thou shalt have joy and gladness: and many shall rejoice at his birth.

For he shall be great in the sight of the Lord, and shall drink neither wine nor strong drink; and he shall be filled with the Holy Ghost, even from his mother's womb.

And many of the children of Israel shall he turn to the Lord their God.

And he shall go before him in the spirit and power of Elias, to turn the hearts of the fathers to the children. . .(Luke 1:13-17).

God called John the Baptist to herald the King and the Kingdom, preparing the way for Israel's Messiah. As our Lord said of John, in Matthew 11:10, *This is he, of whom it is written, Behold I send my messenger before thy face, who shall prepare thy way before thee.* And in Matthew 11:14, the Lord said, in vindication of John who was then in prison: *And if ye will receive it, this is Elias, who is to come.*

In these verses of Scripture taken from the Gospels of Matthew, Mark and Luke there is reference to the three prophecies of the Old Testament concerning the forerunner, John the Baptist. These are: Isaiah 40:3; Malachi 3:1; 4:5,6. That John the Baptist was sent in fulfillment of these prophecies is, therefore, unquestionable.

And his disciples asked him, saying, Why then say the scribes that Elias [Elijah] must first come? And Jesus answered and said unto them, Elias truly shall first come, and restore all things. But I say unto you, That Elias is come already, and they knew him not, but have done unto him whatsoever they listed. . .Then the disciples understood that he spoke unto them of John the Baptist (Matthew 17:10-13).

When the people of Israel refused to heed John's message and did not receive the Lord as their Messiah but rather cried, "Crucify Him," they made it impossible for Him to "restore all things" unto them according to His promise. Therefore, Malachi's prophecy concerning the coming of Elijah to Israel (or one who will come in his spirit and power), awaits a greater, and still future fulfillment which will take place just before our Lord's second coming. It is then, just prior to the Lord's return to the earth, that Elijah's mission will be accomplished among Israel—that of turning the hearts of the fathers to the children, and the hearts of the children to their fathers, and making ready a people prepared for the Lord.

Study to shew thyself approved unto God a workman that needeth not to be ashamed, rightly dividing the word of truth (II Timothy 2:15).

THE BIBLE AND BAPTIZING THE DEAD

As we have said, the Mormon people go to great lengths to trace their genealogy and then by proxy baptism they "save the dead." By misconstruing I Corinthians 15:29, to support their doctrine of baptism for the dead, they would have us believe that the early Christians practiced this ritual in behalf of their dead.

The subject, however, in I Corinthians 15 is the resurrection. But there were some in the church at Corinth, who did not believe in the resurrection. The Apostle Paul said (I Corinthians 15:12) . . .*how say some among you that there is no resurrection of the dead?* Then in the following verses he shows by implication what was involved, *if Christ had not risen.* Finally he asks them the question in verse 29, *Else what shall they do which are baptized for the dead, if the dead rise not at all? why are they then baptized for the dead?*

In other words, they were baptizing over their dead ones and yet, while practicing this ritual, they denied the resurrection. Paul could further say to them, "It does not make sense. Why then baptize for (over) the dead?"

Robert L. Farrier, who has done missionary work among the Mormon people, wrote:

. . . Missionaries from foreign countries, are unanimous in stating, that sprinkling over the dead has been traditionally passed from one generation to another in foreign lands, even though a wide variation of elements have been employed, anywhere from incense to blood.

. . . The Bible has something to say about sprinkling water over a body or over a grave.

Moses, speaking to the people of Israel, in matters of purification, says to them, *And a clean person shall take hyssop and dip it in the water [not blood] and sprinkle it upon the tent, and upon all the vessels, and the persons that were there, and upon him that toucheth a bone, or one slain, or one dead, or a grave*(Numbers 19:18).

There you have it:

Sprinkle the Water Upon one Dead!
Sprinkle the Water Upon one Grave!

Can we not contemplate that this is the origin of the custom dating back to B.C. 1452, and, if the Apostle Paul wrote to the Corinthians in A.D. 59, we have an observance being practiced for a period of approximately 1500 years, having passed over from the Jew to the Greek.

Finally, I Corinthians 15:29 we believe is translated correctly as:

"Seeing this, why perform baptism over the dead, if the dead rise not at all? Why do you then baptize over them now dead?"

At the very beginning of Paul's letter to the Corinthians he wrote, *For Christ sent me not to baptize but to preach the gospel...*
If baptism were a saving ordinance, for this Church Age, could you imagine Paul saying, *I thank God that I have not been instrumental in bringing salvation to you (living or dead).*
The remarks by Harry Bultema in his book, *"The Bible and Baptism,"* on I Corinthians 1:14-17, would be helpful.

The thanksgiving of the Apostle Paul is most significant, when we come to analyze it in this connection. First, it shows that Paul never commanded water baptism for it would have been utterly anomalous and even preposterous first to command a rite and then to glory that he did not keep it. . . .

Then, it clearly disproves the false doctrine of baptismal regeneration, for in that case Paul would have gloried that there were not any, or at least not many, regenerated, and this would have made his thanksgiving positively wicked. . . .It was stated rule and principle with our Apostle never to forsake a truth for the abuse of that truth.

The late Dr. Donald Grey Barnhouse, wrote on the subject of "Baptizing for the Dead" in *Eternity Magazine* (Oct. 1951).

I could think of few methods that would be greater money-makers than a ceremony which would allow a person to be baptized with water at a considerable fee, for the sake of some departed loved one. So far as I know, only the Mormons have established this practice as a rite.

IX

Defense Before the Mormon Bishop's Court

Shortly after I became a Christian, I went to the Mormon Bishop of our Ward and asked him to remove my name from the church rolls because I no longer considered myself a Mormon.

I explained to the bishop that I had been saved by the grace of God and realized now that the Mormon people were not teaching the true Gospel of Christ. I could no longer believe in Mormonism.

One of my uncles, however, heard of the matter and insisted that my name remain on the rolls of the Mormon Church. He was certain I would soon discover my mistake and would be eager to return to the fold. I did not press the matter. *What's the difference?* I thought. *My name is recorded in heaven.*

A few years passed. One day when I was living in Pasadena, California, I received a telephone call from Bishop James C. Ellsworth of the Pasadena Mormon Ward. He asked me if he could come to my home for an interview. I cordially welcomed him.

When the Mormon official arrived he showed me some pamphlets I had written about my conversion from Mormonism and also an article in the local newspaper announcing a meeting where I was speaking on the subject, "From Mormonism to Christ."

"I have written to Utah and discovered that you are still considered to be a Mormon. How is this?" Bishop Ellsworth wanted to know.

I explained that an uncle had intervened when I asked that my name be removed from the church records. I assured the good Mormon that I definitely did not consider myself any longer a member of the Church of Jesus Christ of Latter Day Saints.

After further discussion, Bishop Ellsworth decided that I should be formally excommunicated from the Mormon Church, since I no longer believed in the religion of Mormonism. I agreed, so we set a date for my appearance before the Mormon Bishop's Court.

A Christian friend who also had been converted out of Mormonism became alarmed. "This is a very serious thing for Mormons. You should give it deep consideration and prepare what you want to say in court."

"Of course," I replied. "I'll pray about it."

At that time I was giving a series of Bible studies on the Second Coming of Christ. One Saturday night, after my family had retired for the evening, I was studying chapter 21 of the Gospel of Luke in relation to the tribulation period and Christ's return. I began reading verses 12 through 15. I had not been thinking about my day in court or about what I should say before the Mormon Bishop's Court. But the Holy Spirit made a clear application of these verses to my heart. God seemed to speak to me, saying, "Settle it in your heart not to meditate before what you shall answer, for I will give you a mouth and wisdom which all your adversaries shall not be able to gainsay nor resist."

In verse 13, I had the same assurance that this was for me, "I shall turn to you for a testimony."

I knew with certainty that God had given me the answer to my questions concerning the Bishop's Court. God had spoken to me through His Word. I had great peace in my heart and total confidence in the Lord's promise and was obedient to the Word in not making any preliminary preparation for what I would say in court. Confident that I would be given an opportunity to witness for Christ, I awaited eagerly the hour for my appearance.

The Sunday afternoon arrived, and at two-thirty p.m. I found myself being ushered into the official chamber. No one but my wife was permitted to accompany me. The court was set up in the Mormon Church Ward, and Bishop Ellsworth with two counselors were seated behind their bench.

At each side of the room there was a young man and a young woman with stenotypes ready to take down every word that was spoken.

Bishop Ellsworth opened the session. Evidence was presented before the court, such as articles I had written and newspaper advertisements regarding my meetings. The men asked questions which I answered directly. Soon I was to be excommunicated from the church of my boyhood.

In the course of the investigation, one of the counselors asked for permission to speak to me. Permission was granted, He asked me to reconsider my position, to confirm my belief in Joseph Smith, in the Mormon Church, and to remain true to its teachings.

I thanked the counselor for his concern but explained again that I could no longer believe in the doctrines of the Mormon Church nor was I compatible with the things it stood for. It would be better for all concerned, I felt, if my name was removed officially from the church rolls.

So the court proceeded, and I was then declared to be an "apostate" of the Mormon Church.

Immediately after this action was taken, an amazing opportunity was given to me, as God had assured me there would be, to bear testimony to the saving Gospel of our Lord Jesus Christ. I addressed Bishop Ellsworth:

"In view of the fact that I have come here voluntarily to have my name removed from the records of the Mormon Church, may I speak? I fully realize how serious this is, according to Mormonism, for one to hold the Priesthood and then to renounce it and desire to become an apostate, so I request a little time to tell you why I have taken this step."

Bishop Ellsworth looked at his two counselors and replied, "I see no reason why we should not allow it."

I proceeded boldly to give my testimony. I told the people present that I was baptized when I was eight years old and ordained to the Aaronic Priesthood when I was twelve, and that I had believed in Mormonism with all my heart. I explained that after I left Utah and later in California I had met many types of people of various religions, and that I used to thank God that I belonged to the Mormon religion.

Then I explained how, through the testimony of a young man whose spirituality greatly impressed me, I was persuaded to attend a meeting where I heard the Gospel of salvation through Christ alone. I told them I accepted the grace of God and that Christ became my Savior. I testified how God completely changed my life as I began to study the Bible. I soon discovered that I could no longer go on in the Mormon faith.

By this time, the young man and woman had stopped taking down my words on their stenotypes, straining to catch every word as if it were manna from heaven. I proceeded with my testimony until Bishop Ellsworth asked, "What about the angel flying in the midst of heaven having the everlasting gospel to preach unto them that dwell on the earth?"

The Mormon people associate this event with young Joseph Smith on his knees in the woods asking God to reveal to him the truth of all the sects—which one was the true one that he should join. The Mormons claim that later God sent an angel, Moroni, as though in further answer to Joseph Smith's prayer.

I reminded Bishop Ellsworth that this event was really taken from the fourteenth chapter of Revelation, the sixth verse, but that according to the New Testament account this angel is only one of the many angels whom John saw. The Apostle said: "And I saw another angel." I repeated for him verses eight and nine: *Other angels followed pronouncing their messages* as did the one in verse six. I pointed out that this event had never taken place, that it was all still in the future. What John saw and described for us is all to take place during a specific period called the "Great Tribulation," which will commence after the rapture of the Church. It is during this time of great distress, when the anti-Christ is to deceive and hold many in his unholy power that the angel of Revelation 14:6 will fly in the midst of heaven delivering his message of hope and warning before the Antichrist issues his proclamation that no one can buy or sell.

I also pointed out that this angel does not come down to earth or commune with anyone.

My answer seemed to satisfy the Bishop so I proceeded to tell freely the simple plan of salvation. I had felt the power of the Holy Spirit through the meeting, and I knew when I had said enough. I was almost ready to ask that every head be bowed, that every eye be closed so I might give an invitation to receive Christ as Savior when I realized where I was and the circumstances of the hour. This was a meeting arranged by my hosts but so intent was the leading of the Spirit and so very real the spiritual response that it was hard to remember that I was the one on trial. Like Stephen, when brought before the High Council of Israel (Acts 7), I felt that my accusers were actually on trial, by the Word of God I had given them. I believe they knew I had brought them the truth.

Finally our meeting closed. The young man and the girl came quickly to my side and shook hands. I gave them some gospel tracts.

I also shook hands with the counselors and then Bishop Ellsworth escorted my wife and me to our car. Meditatively he shook our hands and said, "God bless you, Mr. Anderson." Then he turned and went back to his office.

I have never seen any of those people since that day. But when I get to heaven I will not be surprised to find some of them there, because whenever the gospel is preached, some will believe and be saved.

"And some believed the things which were spoken, and some believed not (Acts 28:24).

X

Joseph Smith's Successor

AN IMPORTANT NEW DOCUMENT COMES TO LIGHT

The Mormon Church claims that Joseph Smith was appointed by God to be President of the true church and that there has been an unbroken chain of succession in the Presidency ever since that time. According to Mormon apologists, any break in the chain of succession would throw the church into a state of apostasy.

One of the chief differences between the Mormon Church and the Reorganized Church of Latter Day Saints centers around the question of who was the successor to Joseph Smith. While the Utah Mormons claim that Brigham Young was the true successor, the RLDS maintain that Joseph Smith had bestowed this right on his son Joseph Smith III. Although the Utah Church has always disputed this claim, a recent discovery by Mark Hofmann proves that Joseph Smith actually did designate his son as successor. The Mormon Church's own newspaper, *The Deseret News,* confirmed the authenticity of the document:

> A handwritten document thought to be a father's blessing given by Joseph Smith Jr., first president and prophet of The Church of Jesus Christ of Latter-day Saints, to his son Joseph Smith III, has been acquired by the Church Historical Department.
>
> The document, which includes the possibility of Joseph Smith III succeeding his father as prophet and church leader, was presented Thursday to authorities of the Reorganized Church of Jesus Christ of Latter Day Saints in exchange for another valuable church document.
>
> The artifacts were exchanged at offices of the Church Historical Department with Earl E. Olson, assistant managing director of LDS Church Historical Department, Donald T. Schmidt, Church Archivist, and Richard P Howard, RLDS Church Historian participating. . . .
>
> Olson and other LDS officials said they are convinced the blessing is authentic. Handwriting and the paper were examined and compared with other documents. . . .

The blessing document, dated Jan. 17, 1844, is thought to have been written by Thomas Bullock, one of several men who served as clerk to Joseph Smith Jr. . . .

Church officials obtained the document from Mark William Hofmann, a collector of historical documents and antiques. He said he received it from a descendant of Thomas Bullock. Church officials declined to say how much was paid for the document. . . .

The document outlines a blessing given by Joseph Smith Jr. to his son, then age 11, and includes the possibility of the son succeeding his father "to the Presidency of the High Priesthood: A Seer, and a Revelator, and a Prophet, unto the Church. (Deseret News, March 19, 1981).

The text of the blessing reads as follows:

A blessing, given to Joseph Smith, III, by his father, Joseph Smith, Jr., on Jan. 17, 1844.

Blessed of the Lord is my son Joseph, who is called the third, for the Lord knows the integrity of his heart and loves him, because of his faith and righteous desires. And, for this cause, has the Lord raised him up; that the promises made to the fathers might be fulfilled, even the anointing of the progenitor shall be upon the head of my son, and his seed after him, from generation to generation. For he shall be my successor to the Presidency of the High Priesthood: a Seer, and a Revelator, and a Prophet, unto the Church; which appointment belongeth to him by blessing, and also by right.

Verily, thus saith the Lord: if he abides in me, his days shall be lengthened upon the earth, but if he abides not in me, I, the Lord, will receive him, in an instant, unto myself.

When he is grown, he shall be a strength to his brethren, and a comfort to his mother. Angels will minister unto him, and he will be wafted as on eagle's wings, and be as wise as serpents, even a multiplicity of blessings shall be his. Amen.

THE TRUE SUCCESSOR?

If there is any truth to the claim that Joseph Smith was led by revelation, the blessing given to his son would seem to indicate that Joseph Smith III was the true successor and that Brigham Young wrongfully appropriated this right to himself. The idea that Brigham Young had stolen Joseph Smith's son's right to be President of the Church was widely discussed in the 1800's. John D. Lee, who followed Brigham Young west, made these revealing comments in a book published in 1877:

Every exertion was made to push forward the completion of the Temple at Nauvoo.

Before proceeding further, we must learn who was to be the successor of the Prophet to lead the Church. It was then understood among the Saints that young Joseph was to succeed his father, and that right justly belonged to him. Joseph, the Prophet, had bestowed that right upon him by ordination, but he was too young at that time to fill the office and discharge its solemn duties. Someone must fill the place until he had grown to more mature age . . . a conference was held . . . Brigham Young arose and roared like a young lion, imitating the style and voice of Joseph, the Prophet. Many of the brethren declared that they saw the mantle of Joseph fall upon him. I myself, at the time, imagined that I saw and heard a strong resemblance to the Prophet in him, and felt that he was the man to lead us until Joseph's legal successor should grow up to manhood, when he should surrender the Presidency to the man who held the birthright. After that time, if he continued to claim and hold the position, he could not be considered anything else than an usurper, and his acts would not meet the approbation of Heaven. Hence the course of Brigham Young has been downward ever since. . . .

I heard Mother Smith, the mother of Joseph, the Prophet, plead with Brigham Young, with tears, not to rob young Joseph of his birthright, which his father, the Prophet, bestowed upon him previous to his death; that young Joseph was to succeed his father as the leader of the Church; and that it was his right in the line of the priesthood. "I know it," replied Brigham, "don't worry or take any trouble, Mother Smith; by so doing you are only laying the knife to the throat of the child. If it is known that he is the rightful successor of his father, the enemy of the Priesthood will seek his life. He is too young to lead this people now, but when he arrives at mature age he shall have his place. No one shall rob him of it." This conversation took place in the Masonic Hall at Nauvoo, in 1845. Several persons were then present.

In the meantime Brigham had sought to establish himself as the leader of this Church. Many years, however, passed away before he dared assume or claim to be the rightful successor of Joseph, the Seer, Prophet, and Revelator to the Church. When the time came, according to his own words, for Joseph to receive his own, Joseph came, but Brigham received him not. He said, as an excuse, that Joseph had not the true spirit, that his mother had married a Gentile lawyer and had infused the Gentile spirit into him, and that Joseph denied the doctrine of his father—celestial marriage. Brigham closed the door and barred him from preaching in the Tabernacle, and raised a storm of persecution against him.

He took Joseph's cousin, George A. Smith, as his first counselor. This he did as a matter of policy to prevent George A. from using his influence in favor of Joseph as the leader of the people, which he otherwise would have done. He also ordained John Smith, the son of Hyrum the Patriarch, to the office of Patriarch to the Church, and his brother Joseph F. Smith, to the office of one of the Twelve Apostles, thus securing their influence and telling them that had young Joseph been willing to act in harmony with them, the heads of the

Church, he could have had his place, but that he was too much a Gentile ever to lead this people.

Brigham said he had some hopes that David, a brother of young Joseph, when he became older, might occupy the place of his father, but Joseph never would. In this low, cunning, intriguing way, he blinded the eyes of the people and gained another advantage over them in establishing himself and family at the head of the Church, as the favored of the Lord.... I remember twenty years ago, among the first members of the Church, it was all the talk that young Joseph would take the leadership of the Church, as the rightful successor of his father, the Prophet.

At that time it never was thought that Brigham Young intended to hold the place permanently.... The Saints have suffered themselves to be led step by step downward, lulled to sleep by false promises and phantoms that can never be realized. (*Mormonism Unveiled; Or The Life And Confessions Of the Late Mormon Bishop,* John D. Lee, St. Louis, 1877, Pages 155, 156, 161, 162 and 164.)

In 1855 George Miller wrote a letter which informs that, just after Joseph Smith's death, the Mormon leaders claimed to have "sealed documents" which would settle the succession question:

On my arrival in Nauvoo, I visited Elder John Taylor, of the quorum of the Apostles, who was sick of his wounds received in Carthage jail, at the time of Joseph's death. Dr. Willard Richards was there, and after a few remarks in regard to the mob, I asked him who Joseph had left to succeed him in the prophetic office. He replied that all was right; that there were sealed documents left, which would be opened when the twelve Apostles should get home that would settle all these matters. Sidney Rigdon had already returned from Pittsburgh (where he was sent before Joseph's death), and had made some moves as a leader of the people, and from hints and inuendos that I heard frequently I was induced to believe that Joseph had designated his son to succeed him in the prophetic office, and on this belief I rested....

Subsequent to these times of intense excitement I had frequent attempts at conversation with Brigham Young and H. C. Kimball in regard to Joseph's leaving one to succeed him in the prophetic office, and in all my attempts to ascertain the desired truth as to that personage, I was invariably met with the inuendo, 'stop,' or 'hush' Brother Miller, let there be nothing said in regard to this matter, or we will have little Joseph killed as his father was, inferring indirectly that Joseph Smith had appointed his son Joseph to succeed him in the prophetic office, and I believe this impression was not alone left on my mind, but on the brethren in general, and remains with many until this day. (Correspondence of Bishop George Miller with *The Northern Islander,* pages 22-23).

WHAT DOES IT ALL MEAN?

Since the recently discovered blessing provides devastating evidence against the Utah Mormon Church, officials from the Church have tried to downplay its importance. According to the Salt Lake Tribune, March 20, 1981, Church spokesman Jerry Cahill referred to it only as "an interesting historical footnote." Members of the RLDS Church, on the other hand, are elated over the discovery:

> ... in Independence, the RLDS Church statement read in part:
>
> The prayer of blessing of Joseph Smith Jr. designating his son, Joseph Smith III, to be his successor in the prophetic office of the church confirms the historical view long held by members of the RLDS Church.

We cannot believe that all this confusion could possibly come from the Lord. The Bible says that "God is not the author of confusion" (I Corinthians 14:33). It would appear from the evidence presented that if the Mormon Church ever had any "priesthood," it was lost when Brigham Young took the presidency unto himself.

Excerpts used by permission from Tanners' book, *Joseph Smith's Successor*, available from Modern Microfilm Co., P.O. Box 1881, Salt Lake City, Utah 84110.

The Reorganized Church of Latter Day Saints with headquarters in Independence, Missouri, rejects the designation Mormon, and, at present, uses the terms: The Saints Church, Reorganized Latter Day Saints or simply The Saints. The United States government has decided, at least once, that the RLDS Church has the best claim to the succession.

The Church of Christ, with headquarters in Independence, Missouri, sometimes referred to as the Temple Lot Mormons, claims to be the true Mormon Church by reason of the fact that it is in possession of the piece of ground that Joseph Smith designated as the site of the Temple of Zion that is to be built on this lot before the Second Advent of Christ.